AIT OF THE MANAGER
OUNG AUTHOR

UNTIMELY MEDITATIONS

PORTRAIT OF THE MANAGER AS A YOUNG AUTHOR

ON STORYTELLING, BUSINESS, AND LITERATURE

PHILIPP SCHÖNTHALER

TRANSLATED BY AMANDA DEMARCO

THE MIT PRESS
CAMBRIDGE, MASSACHUSETTS
LONDON, ENGLAND

First published as *Porträt des Managers als junger Autor. Zum Verhältnis von Wirtschaft und Literatur* in the series *Fröhliche Wissenschaft* at Matthes & Seitz Berlin: © MSB Matthes & Seitz Berlin Verlagsgesellschaft mbH, Berlin 2016. All rights reserved.

The translation of this work was supported by a grant from the Goethe-Institut in the framework of the "Books First" program.

This book was set in PF DinText Pro by Toppan Best-set Premedia Limited. Printed and bound in the United States of America.

Library of Congress Cataloging-in-Publication Data

Names: Schönthaler, Philipp, author.
Title: Portrait of the manager as a young author : on storytelling, business, and
    literature / Philipp Schönthaler ; translated by Amanda DeMarco.
Other titles: Portrait des Managers als junger Autor. English | Storytelling, business,
    and literature
Description: Cambridge, MA : MIT Press, 2018. | Series: Untimely meditations ; 12 |
    First published in German in 2016. | Includes bibliographical references.
Identifiers: LCCN 2018002501 | ISBN 9780262535748 (pbk. : alk. paper)
Subjects: LCSH: Economics and literature. | Storytelling.
Classification: LCC PT2720.064 P6713 2018 | DDC 833/.92--dc23 LC record available
at https://lccn.loc.gov/2018002501

ISBN: 978-0-262-53574-8

10 9 8 7 6 5 4 3 2 1

CONTENTS

CONTENTS

Agency storefront on Sunset
Boulevard in Los Angeles

Narrative remains largely unconcerned with good or bad literature. Like life itself, it is there, international, transhistorical, transcultural.

—Roland Barthes

I am honored to be with you today at your commencement from one of the finest universities in the world. I never graduated from college. Truth be told, this is the closest I've ever gotten to a college graduation. Today I want to tell you three stories from my life. That's it. No big deal. Just three stories.

—Introductory words of Steve Jobs's Stanford commencement address on June 12, 2005

PORTRAIT OF THE MANAGER AS A YOUNG AUTHOR

I AT THE HEART OF STORYTELLING: NINE SKETCHES FROM THEORY AND PRACTICE

TAKE YOUR TIME

Narrative and management: in management storytelling, the two concepts forge an alliance that demands a bit of explanation. Management is governed by pragmatism. Its aim is rationalization, decision making, and goal-oriented action, and what counts is the balance left at the end. Narrative, on the other hand, requires room to breathe. Primary concerns come second to secondary ones, fact second to fiction. Its message is ambiguous at best. The economy of narrative, which always favors diversion, clashes with technological modernity's law of acceleration, a law that governs businesses directly. The philosopher Hans Blumenberg wrote that stories are told in order to pass time and dispel fear, which hardly speaks to the concerns of managers, whose decision making and actions are based on the fact that time is limited. A day in the life of a manager is tightly scheduled, dominated by interruptions and variety, with utterly paradoxical results: "I don't have time for time management," says a manager, who has worked on the problem with coaches, trainers, and handbooks.[1]

But management storytelling isn't on the defensive. On the contrary, it promotes narrative as the privileged form of communication for organizations. In fact, the names of the international corporations and institutions that have worked with storytelling methods speak for themselves: IBM, Nike, Ford, Shell, Coca-Cola, World Bank, Federal Express, Tipp-Ex, Danone, Renault. For many years, Procter & Gamble advertised a position for a corporate storyteller. At Microsoft, Steve Clayton is currently chief storyteller on a team of twenty-five corporate storytellers. One of their projects from 2015 included a science fiction story collection, which the company hired science fiction authors to write. The German list hardly lags behind: Deutsche Post World Net, Siemens (in cooperation with Ludwig-Maximilian University of Munich), T-Mobile, Bosch, voestalpine Steel, the sensor manufacturer Sick, F.A.S.T (Society for Applied Software Technology).

The presence on this list of a company like F.A.S.T., which asserts the ideology of digital media in its very name, raises the question of how traditional narrative can be compatible with new information and communication technologies in their heightened form. At F.A.S.T., narrative methods are implemented to restructure internal communications processes, as well as in project management. The Munich-based corporation now belongs to Cirquent, a consulting firm for IT and technologically supported organization processes; since 2012, the latter in turn has belonged to NTT Data, a Japanese business responsible for establishing the entire structure of payment by credit card in Japan and a trendsetter in the field of big data. According to the literature, storytelling gains its legitimation precisely where digital information flows too quickly, exceeding the cognitive capacity of the human brain and leaving the data too abstract for its practical value to be identifiable without further assistance. The recourse to narrative as an established practice arises not out of desperation but in answer to the "hard" criteria of management: efficiency and effectiveness. Precisely because digital information technologies outstrip human powers of comprehension and the rhythms of human cognition, new media do not replace old media but rather integrate them. They represent neither skepticism toward technology, nor regression, nor nostalgia. Instead, narrative beats digital communications technology on its own turf of optimized information processing and circulation.

LONG LIVE THE KING

Narrative has always regulated our approach to complexity. In this function, it has recently become attractive to modern societies, which generally define themselves through processes of differentiation. According to the French sociologist and philosopher Jean Baudrillard, in the course of digitalization and virtualization, late capitalist society—led by the world of finance—entered a stage of hypercomplexity beginning in the 1970s. The reemergence of storytelling can thus be interpreted as a reaction to a new obscurity. Narrative, as it were, displays a perfect degree of complexity, surpassing the critical threshold of "pure" data in this respect. Pure data is constantly accumulating in the information age and lacks its own logical value as such, proving to be as difficult to consume as to remember. At the same time, narrative goes beyond the tremendous speed and abstraction of the electronic flow of information. Though the quantitative information contained in narratives proves relatively modest, narratives generate strong powers of identification and integration. Since, as a medium for knowledge, narrative undergoes few specialization processes, it represents a highly accessible form of communication with a low threshold for connection.

With regard to the coalition of narrative and management, dealing with complexity is built into the task of the manager. Managers owe their existence to earlier advances in rationalization and differentiation processes, which led to a crisis—generally described as a crisis in communication—in the second half of the nineteenth century. With the emergence of larger firms, the organization of work became a problem in itself. The new position of the salaried manager was supposed to counteract the resulting problems of large modern businesses; within accelerated production and distribution processes, coordination and communication take first priority. As a consequence, the figure of the manager is a product of complexity, while the manager's task consists of overcoming complexity. In this function, they fall back on narrative because they know that precisely within confusing, speed-oriented communications structures, "people are the most important factor for the success of the business," as the organization scholar and Narrata Consult founder Karin Thier explains in her book, *Storytelling: A Narrative Management Method.*[2] Storytelling proves to be a superior communication technique whenever people are involved in information and communication cycles as affective and cognitive beings.

The chief executive of F.A.S.T. had exactly the same experience: "F.A.S.T. is a heavily project-driven business, which is why it's essential for us to make use of soft knowledge within project work and to constantly improve it. But until now, we didn't have a method to do so." Storytelling now meets these needs: "I could imagine," the CEO continued, "that in the future, storytelling will become a regular feature of our CIP [Continual Improvement Process] within the scope of quality management in accordance with ISO 9001. In any case, F.A.S.T. would like to work more with storytelling methods in the future."

On this point, storytelling scholarship delivers striking findings. The philosopher and literary critic Walter Benjamin conjured the figure of the oral storyteller in the first half of the twentieth century, only to definitively place it in the past. For Benjamin, information and narrative are irreconcilable; information goes hand-in-hand with a desire for factuality and verifiability, driving out the spirit of narrative, with its claim to truth based in lifeworld experience. Thus, Benjamin comes to the conclusion that the incipient information society will put an end to the narrator and to narration.[3] Eighty years after Benjamin's diagnosis, storytelling is heading in precisely the opposite direction, witnessing the return of the oral storyteller—right in the heart of information production.

TWO ARTISTS IN PARIS

Hans Christian Andersen's fairy tale "The Emperor's New Clothes" still fascinates us. It does so above all because it satisfies our regressive impulse to disrobe a "naked" truth, especially because the story is about a ruler who disregards the good of his people. In the fairy tale, this urge is represented by the "innocent" child who reveals the nakedness of the emperor, and with it the chicanery of the royal court.[4] Although it is possible to read the story in solidarity with the weavers, Andersen's narrator denounces them throughout as swindlers. In this sense he is like a child who demands a one-dimensional truth. Ultimately, he also weaves his narration from the sole motivation of revealing the emperor in his nakedness, replicating precisely what he accuses the weavers of doing. The fictive texture of the fairy tale exposes the emperor and his refinement, just as the weaver's textiles do. Unlike the weavers, Andersen's narrator misjudges the two bodies of the emperor, whose power remains invisible because it is symbolic and is effective only because of the social dynamics of recognition and dependency. From the weavers' point of view, the child and the narrator are stupid because they prove themselves to be blind to the imaginary and fictional origins and structures of political and institutional power. The weavers' fictive garments actually deliver on their promise: they're not just artful, they also unmask those who lack the ability to distinguish the real from the symbolic—in this case the child and the narrator, in their blindness to the symbolic nature of power. However, the fairy tale exhibits another layer, which consists in the curious fact that the emperor's disrobing has no consequences: "'This procession has got to go on,'" the emperor thinks after he has been exposed, and walks more proudly than ever. The ceremony takes its course, and the ending of the fairy tale remains open.

Andersen's story is set in a royal court. Accordingly, its first point of reference is the mechanics of political and symbolic power. Moreover, the story testifies to a general logic that can also be applied to other fields. Just as political power is symbolically charged, so are the value and power of products and companies. This is particularly true of what the French sociologists Luc Boltanski and Arnaud Esquerre recently termed "enrichment capitalism," in order to describe the current trend toward a postindustrial economy where the value of products is "based on narrative projections."[5] With this in mind, I want to turn to an often told story from Steve Jobs's anecdote-filled career. The episode dates from the eve of the new economy. The Macintosh computer was still in development, and just a generation earlier, Santa Clara County, California, was primarily known for its orchards and prune production, not as Silicon Valley. Management literature usually cites only a single line from the story. It is a sentence that Jobs supposedly used in order to convince John Sculley, marketing expert and then vice president of PepsiCo, to become Apple's new CEO: "Do you really want to sell sugar water, or do you want to come with me and change the world?" As the story goes, this sentence won Sculley over on the spot. He resigned from Pepsi and joined Apple shortly thereafter. The incident is commonly cited as proof of Jobs's charismatic leadership qualities, as an exceptional talent who embodied the promise of the new technology like no other. But there's more to the story than that. The episode is as follows.[6]

It's late 1982, and Apple is looking for a new CEO. The incumbent, Mike Markkula, only accepted his post temporarily, and he wants to step down permanently. The general consensus is that Steve Jobs isn't yet ready to lead the company himself, but he's charged with recruiting. He finally zeroes in on John Sculley, who won the first battle in the cola wars with the Pepsi Challenge and made the company number one in the soft drink industry, ahead of Coca-Cola, just a few years before. Sculley is also taken with the charismatic Jobs, but he sidesteps the offer. Sculley first visits Apple headquarters on the West Coast, then, at a meeting in New York, Jobs presents the new Lisa computer. After a stop at the Hotel Carlyle, they go to the Four Seasons together. Sculley explains his marketing success to Jobs: with the Pepsi Generation campaign, he wasn't selling a product but rather a lifestyle and a positive worldview. The two part ways just before midnight. Jobs is enthused. In his own words, he'd just had "one of the most exciting evenings in my whole life."[7] More meetings follow in which the two grow closer. Jobs visits Sculley at his new country estate in Greenwich, admiring the 300-pound oak doors and eclectic private library. Then they drive a Mercedes SL 450 to a Pepsi branch office. The two businesses could hardly be more different: The redoubtable Pepsi CEO Donald Kendall was still in the habit of having a butler in a white suit jacket attend meetings to serve him Pepsi in a crystal glass on a silver platter, a Havana cigar between his pursed lips. Worlds collide with these two businesses: elite Fortune 500 establishment on the one side, hippyesque DIY economy on the other. Mechanics at Pepsi must follow a dress code completely unknown to Apple management. The decisive meeting finally takes place in March 1983. Sculley, who comes from a well-to-do Upper East Side family—his mother wore white gloves whenever she left the house—brings Jobs to the Metropolitan Museum. He wants to see if this "whiz kid," whom he'll describe in the first sentences of his autobiography, published five years later, as "my closest friend, a soul mate and a constant companion,"[8] is willing to take a few lessons from him on the Old Masters. This is a mandatory test because as CEO, Sculley will actually be Jobs's superior at Apple. After the museum visit, they go for a walk, during which Sculley confides that on vacation he would like to sit on the Left Bank and sketch. Had he not become a manager and marketing expert, he would have been an artist. Sculley has managed to bring the topic around from art appreciation to art production, and lo and behold, the two finally hit it off. Jobs can also imagine himself on the banks of that storied river: had he not become a computer developer, today he would be living as a poet in Paris, he confesses to the artistically inclined soft drink entrepreneur.

The two pay a visit to Colony Records on 49th Street, then stroll all the way back to the San Remo building on the corner of Central Park West and 74th Street, where Jobs wants to buy a condo. On the terrace, Jobs utters the decisive sentence that, anecdote has it, wins Sculley over. It hits the PepsiCo "marketing wizard" like "a stiff blow to my stomach": "Do you really want to sell sugar water, or do you want to come with me and change the world?"[9]

We can use Andersen's fairy tale to decipher this scene. First of all, the roles are clearly assigned: Jobs plays the impertinent child who points to what everyone already knows: Pepsi isn't a lifestyle or a worldview, it's sugar water. Sculley performs the thankless role of the emperor and allows himself to be exposed. His praise for his own marketing strategy, proclaiming just the opposite, hasn't yet faded from memory. With this bit of theater, Sculley and Jobs satisfy their audience's regressive wish for unveiling and simple truths: The good things in life still exist. We can differentiate between the symbolic and the use value of a product anytime.

The two (artist and poet) also simultaneously take up the role of the weavers, espousing the knowledge that businesses and goods actually accrue value from symbolic attributions. That's why the meeting of the two men must be suitably fleshed out before Jobs can unite both conflicting positions (child and weaver) in just one sentence, disqualifying Pepsi as sugar water while enthroning Apple as a project to change the world. Jobs's sentence consolidates the communication strategy that Sculley had just imparted to him in the Four Seasons: if you want to be successful, you can't just sell products, you have to sell a lifestyle, a positive worldview. Sculley's ruse lies in allowing himself to be exposed by Jobs. Honestly, he probably had an inkling that he would once again be elevated in his position at Apple.

To recognize how the encounter between Jobs and Sculley can be read against the script of Andersen's fairy tale, it is only necessary to understand one twist. Anderson's tale falls into three phases: conjuring illusion, unveiling, and precarious transitions between the two points. These phases form a single process that is dynamic in its chronology, resulting in a general formula that can be represented as a simple chain: disillusion—transition—illusion. As an illusion-machine, this chain is based on the insight that an illusion can only be effectively created on the ground of a prior disillusion. Because the symbolic value of a product (such as power) isn't based on difference alone (emperor versus subject, name brand versus generic product) but also on a hierarchy, the act of symbolic value creation is most easily accomplished by means of an unveiling. In the world of commodities, this process may be carried out on a prior model that is replaced by a new one and is now therefore identified as inadequate, but it can also be applied to the competition or to an abstract value. When Sculley, as the future CEO of Apple, took up the shameful position of the naked emperor in order to shift the company and its founder-hero into the limelight, he demonstrated how to effectively fire up the illusion machine for which Andersen had delivered the blueprints. As in the case of Andersen's weavers, the creation of its narrative fabric depended on the act of conjuring, not only on the subsequent demystification that is Jobs's declaration.

Sculley and Jobs's working relationship was a brief one, but Sculley's ingenious marketing strategy, perfected by Jobs, helps shed some light on the doubtful situation of Steve Jobs's successor, Tim Cook. When Cook presented the "new generation" of products on September 9, 2014, he had already been CEO for four years. The climax was the unveiling of the new Apple Watch, which was to inaugurate "the next chapter in *Apple's story*" as "one of the most influential technology firms in the world," according to Cook in his speech. By the close of that day, the company's market price had sunk by 0.38 percent. All of the observers, from investors to fans, from finance papers to lifestyle magazines, saw him only as a pale imitation of Jobs, indicating that Apple had less of a technological problem on its hands with Cook than a communications one. And in fact, the claim to "revolutionary innovation" that was supposed to open a new chapter in Apple's history doesn't sound very credible, but it comes in precisely the garb that Jobs used for styling himself as an icon. The stage in the Flint Center in Cupertino, California, that Cook chose for the presentation is the same stage from which Jobs launched the Macintosh computer in 1984, inaugurating Apple's global success. Even Cook's gestures imitated the sneaker-wearing prophet, both arms raised victoriously in praise of his own products. Cook introduced the "revolutionary product" with the phrase "One more thing," a tic that was characteristic of Jobs's lapidary product announcements. In an exclusive interview with Cook about launching the watch, we learn that Jobs's office on the fourth floor of the corporate headquarters has been kept just as it was before his death. His nameplate still graces the door. As it turns out, the revolution will be mummified.

Here, Andersen's fairy tale also provides insight: Cook finds himself in the precarious position of the naked emperor among the people. Even the motto he uses as he attempts to carry on Jobs's legacy precisely mirrors the emperor's posture during the ceremony: "This procession has got to go on." Of course, the irony lies in the fact that Andersen's emperor suffered an exposure, while all fingers are pointed at Cook because he's incapable of conjuring a convincing illusion—which is what the audience expects. The future of the business depends on whether Cook will eventually find such artistically inclined weavers as once fashioned the emperor's clothing. In other words, is it possible to build on Jobs's legacy as a storyteller rather than a technologist? "Today I want to tell you three stories from my life," the entrepreneur said in his speech to the Stanford Class of 2005. At that point, he was at the peak of his game, and technology had long been a matter of lifestyle: "That's it. No big deal. Just three stories."[10]

THE MAGIC OF SYMPATHY

The birth of business storytelling is date-stamped. In the mid-1990s at the Center for Organizational Learning at MIT, a network of researchers, journalists, and managers from several companies (including Shell, Philips, Hewlett-Packard, AT&T, and Harley-Davidson) began exploring storytelling as a method with a scientific basis. This occurred within the context of the "learning organization"—a company that is constantly transforming, and that encourages its employees to adapt as well—an influential model in business economics and organizational theory at the time. The learning historian pioneers' group at MIT set itself the goal of investigating collective learning processes, especially documenting and disseminating their findings, so that the learning processes of individuals or groups could be better used in the organization as a whole. The story proved to be the optimal medium for gathering and working through the pioneer group's learning processes within the business, including their expectations, experiences, and mistakes. To this end, the researchers developed the "jointly told tale," "in which participants and outside observers tell the story side-by-side."[11] This collective processing and narrative form, which is derived from ethnological techniques, forms the substance of the "learning story"—the concept that was supposed to lend companies a history and relatability, which subsequently can be acted on. Originally in this model, the story was mainly supposed to function internally, as a way of integrating employees into the business, but it quickly was also used to present the business outwardly, toward customers, for example.

The aim of corporate storytelling as a medium for internal communication has less to do with anchoring the organization in the past (as in marketing, in which the business is linked to its history and thus valorized) and more to do with orienting it toward an uncertain future in a way that is flexible and promotes learning. Businesses are no longer conceived of as static units or as metaphorical containers but rather—as in cybernetics or in Niklas Luhmann's systems theory—as constant communication and decision-making processes. From a pragmatic point of view, the "learning history" approach arises from the challenge of reorganizing or fusing businesses. But the use of storytelling extends beyond that: storytelling can be used to analyze the weaknesses of various parts of an organization, to mobilize untapped resources, or to unite employees in a common business culture and set of values. In this model, everyone is a potential storyteller, managers as well as staff. But not all stories are created equal; spontaneous testimonials that limn how employees perceive their company and work have little in common with an official address in which the manager aligns staff on a unified course in order to integrate them into the business.

The "learning history" approach, however, explicitly distills its method from the consolidation of both aspects. Though storytelling first gained popularity outside the Center for Organizational Learning, the center's success rested on transforming storytelling into an art and a method with certain rules and contrivances, ones that could be learned and that allowed storytellers to differentiate between better and worse narrative modes in pursuing a specific objective. What's more, storytelling may not come with a guarantee, but it does promise to connect people with others. As such, it pursues the dream of absolutely efficacious communication, which it elevates to the first lesson of narration: *tell stories that draw people in.*

A REPORT FOR THE SHAREHOLDERS

At the Daimler AG annual general meeting on April 9, 2014, at the ICC exhibition center in Berlin, the chairman of the board and leader of Mercedes-Benz Cars gave a speech that went on for more than forty-five minutes.[12] The essence of the talk had much in common with the chairman's legendary walrus mustache: its tremendous stolidity, the quintessence of intransigence. Dieter Zetsche's appearance is disconcerting because it seems to contradict the company's self-imposed cult of youth, embodied in the vehicles' resemblance to carnivores; his lectern is flanked by models that seem ready to pounce. Others prowl across the screen behind him as Zetsche drones on in perfect and uninterrupted monotony.

Those present are mainly of a generation for whom this brand represented the German postwar economic boom. Together with his mustache, the three-pointed star of the brand's logo formed the sole remaining link to a recent past in which it was still possible to conceive of automobility without dynamism. The new models have expunged all memory of the days when Mercedes dominated German streets with the art of downtempo driving, from the farmer in a forest-green 240d to the head of state in a black sedan. Back then Mercedes drivers appeared to steer their vehicles unencumbered by any need to get somewhere, taking their cars out of the garage from time to time only to show that they had already arrived.

By 2014 the retrospective extended only to the previous year, and along with the balance sheet and forecast, only the brand's future viability seemed to be of interest. The futuristic design promised to successfully conquer new markets. However, only one moment proved memorable to those present. For the first thirty-two minutes of his speech, the head manager seemed not to suspect that he might curry the shareholders' favor through any other means than facts and figures—no jokes, no irony, no anecdotes. Even successes were rattled off with the same expressionless countenance, without even conceding a smile.

But then the chairman allowed himself a theatrical interlude that was unique in his report, which so far had been free of rhetoric. Its theme was safety, the core of the company's brand. The vehicle safety studies were excellent, "but more impressive than any statistic are the many letters and emails that we receive each year from our customers on the topic of safety." He had brought one of these letters with him, he announced, his right hand sliding into the left interior pocket of his suit coat to pull out a folded letter, which he proceeded to read. Nothing about this moment suggested he was a car enthusiast except the way he held the letter-sized sheet on the left and right, as you would grip a steering wheel. Hardly had he finished the last line when the letter disappeared back into his pocket, near to his heart.

The scene lasted thirty-four seconds. It was utterly unspectacular, but nonetheless noteworthy. Obviously the chairman could simply have continued reading out his speech, which was still lying before him on the lectern. The same lines he read from the letter are printed in cursive script at the point where the speech breaks off. By materially doubling the text, by reaching into his pocket, he made a leap that no one could have expected of him—stepping onto the stage of rhetoric, of theater, and of fiction. The scene is a simple one, but its efficiency, which puts any presentation of statistics to shame, is impressive above all because of the minimal means employed. The letter's content is largely inconsequential. A customer, "Joan," thanked the company because he and his wife survived a "terrible" accident for which they were not at fault, and walked away unscathed thanks to the new CLA. The story told in the letter only repeats what the chairman has documented in a general way just moments before by means of statistics ("the chance of getting in a bad accident in a C Class is forty percent lower on average than in another comparable model.") Apparently, the letter was supposed to communicate something else.

His hand on the left side of his chest alerts us to the fact that we've come to the heart of the speech. All of the numbers, statistics, and strategies are necessary; the shareholders' presence compels the manager to list them. But now he takes half a minute to share a heartfelt matter. That's also why he puts the letter back instead of laying it on the lectern, where it might have slipped between the pages of the speech. The separation of the documents is categorical—and sacred. The one text has nothing to do with the other, though their words are identical. (Incidentally, with this gesture, the chairman forces the attendees to guess what will happen to the letter after the meeting. Will he toss it in the trash? Will he show it to friends or perhaps his wife, or even keep it with other letters in his office or at home— and wouldn't that suggest that he takes it out from time to time in a moment of euphoria or melancholia, and reads it again?) The company's and shareholders' expectations of profitability and the future are also forgotten at this moment;

instead, the focus rests on the all-too-human: following a decisive experience, one person turns to another out of gratitude. One of them happens to be the chairman of a global corporation, and we now learn firsthand that his heart is in the right place: with the customers, who are spread throughout the whole world. The business is massive, and in the next year it wants to gain a greater market share (the return on sales should be 9 percent, the return on equity at least 17 percent), but thanks to this bit of theater, we know that the customers are being heard. That's why the chairman reads the letter. He doesn't want to bring attention to "Joan"; his only concern is demonstrating to the shareholders his own limitless attentiveness, which takes even an individual, insignificant voice like that of "Joan" to heart.

One could write a swan song to the letter in the electronic age. But as early as the 1970s, the influential management researcher Henry Mintzberg had noted that managers aren't fond of letters. As a means of communication they're too slow and unspecific in their directives, displaying "the dullness of a medium that lacks immediate feedback."[13] But in this situation the antiquated medium is superior to any electronic means of communication. In the next phase, the chairman talks about the future of mobility, "Mercedes-Benz Intelligent Drive," and the gradual introduction of autonomous cars. The way it looks, analog culture can celebrate another victory on the ICC stage in Berlin. That's the significance of the letter that's more moving than any email. It's an artifact that's passed through the hands of individual people to connect them in this unique way: the customer, probably Spanish or Mexican but perhaps American, with the chairman. As the chairman shares the letter with the stockholders, they also become the audience and witness to an intimate event whose physical, presence-substantiating quality proves all the more effective in the digital era. The walrus mustache is just a banal stage prop, but during the reading of the anachronistic media it's suddenly just right, nearly making us forget that it's theater we're attending. The shareholders leave the scene completely alert, and with spontaneous applause.

HABITUAL CHANGE

Today management often entails moderating processes of change. Contrary to the claims of those who would scorn managers as mere custodians of the status quo, we can tell that management is a product of capitalism, not least because of their shared will to change. Both Karl Marx and the Austrian economist Joseph Schumpeter identified constant transformation as a characteristic of capitalism's social order. Change management is its own branch of business administration, one whose keywords include "reorganization" and "fusion." But in general, managing also means making processes more efficient, which often entails doing the same thing but differently. Resistance belongs to the nature of change, and typically it is exercised by human creatures of habit. Even measures that are beneficial to everyone meet with the law of inertia and provoke anxiety.

That's why good management must lay the groundwork for change: "The first obstacle to change is getting people to accept that change is needed."[14] This basic tenet of change management is inherent in the first premises of business administration, with its horizontal leadership structures and teamwork. The new approach has less to do with capitalism suffering an access of humanism than the fact that constant sameness demands an escalation of efficiency-oriented thinking, calibrated on productivity and profit. That's because employees only become a "factor for success" if processes of change don't provoke resistance or fear, but rather unleash positive "forces of transformation." "Changemasters have to focus people's eyes on the prize," Rosabeth Moss Kanter, professor at Harvard Business School, repeats her mantra. "To get them to see the value beyond the hardship of change to the prize waiting at the end."[15]

Stories promise to meet these demands because they can simultaneously address fears and desires, consistency and change. Moreover, in the best scenarios, they unify these conflicting emotions and conditions in an ongoing narrative. That's why storytelling can present the prospect of an optimistic outcome: "Stories can be used ... to purposefully direct and influence processes of change in organizations. They represent an instrument that can be strategically used."[16]

Storytelling proves so useful in change management because of the way that narrative is always linked with mutability on a structural level, which is a result of the story's relationship to time. Aristotle's famous characterization of stories as having a beginning, middle, and end not only testifies to the fact that stories evolve through time, it also suggests that there is a transformation taking place that differentiates the endpoint from the beginning. Thus stories organize themselves in the temporal dimension and in doing so, they necessarily deal with change. "Stories are often oriented toward the future, or they're retrospective, linguistic articulations of mutability,"[17] writes the literary critic Albrecht Koschorke, and the consultant Karin Thier says something similar: "Change is the material stories are woven from."[18]

As a medium of transformation, stories play a complex role because on the one hand, a story is structurally extremely conservative. An endless number of stories follow the same plots (satisfying the listeners who—if we believe what neurological studies have to tell us—are also structurally conservative, accepting or even demanding surprises at the level of content but not at the level of the basic formula). On the other hand, stories are also a revolutionary medium because they have the power to subject everything to time and therefore mutability. Narrative management takes advantage of these two aspects, merging them into one unified *story line.* Faced with conservative human tendencies, narrative attests to the necessity of constant change as the oldest law of storytelling (as all the accomplishments of civilization since time immemorial have been accompanied by stories). Management storytelling is characterized by a formulation rather than by a single story: nothing makes mutability easier to moderate than immutable methods. Accordingly, a basic tenet of storytelling is that human beings are *natural-born storytellers*, narrative animals.

A NEW HEART

Futuristic fantasies are often outfitted with archaic elements, as if boldly looking ahead toward the future had to be buffered by recourse to a prehistory. The newest management and marketing methods follow a similar formula. Management storytelling often claims that these methods are among the oldest of practices or natural processes, generally enthroned by neurobiology and brain research. Tham Khai Meng, worldwide chief creative officer at the Ogilvy & Mather Agency (which has done campaigns for Coca-Cola, Nestlé, Yahoo, Greenpeace, and others), designates storytelling as the "holy grail" of successful communication and marketing: "I am sure you've all heard it said that prostitution is the world's oldest profession. But I don't agree. I think that there is an even older one. It is the one we all work in here: storytelling"[19] In an audacious inversion, its seniority is what qualifies narrative as an advanced cultural technique. The stage props for this prehistory are hunting and gathering, along with the fire that the tribe gathers around at night to bond over the narrative act—or according to Tham, the narrative "profession," placing economics squarely in the misty past.

From podiums at Cannes, where the marketing industry meets annually for the Cannes Lions International Festival of Creativity, to the workspaces of global concerns, whose architecture shifts to suit the in-house communication style—for as often as narrative is mentioned, it remains devoid of content. No one seriously expects to shed light on business culture through regression to archaic rites. Nonetheless, the function of this mythical borrowing that narrative management attributes to the story is perfectly clear: capitalism entails processes of alienation and abstraction, which narrative is supposed to counter with images of the community; where social structures and technological developments abrogate the subject's agency, storytelling puts the focus on the fate of the individual. In the midst of the inflationary sensory offerings that circulate throughout the worlds of consumption and goods, the story generates pockets of reenchantment.

Coca-Cola's "Content 2020" strategy, which caused an international sensation in the advertising industry, says that "we must remember that storytelling is at the heart of all families, communities, and cultures," then more or less declares narrative to be the new soul of the cola company.[20] The message is clear. The business is the timeless fire around which consumers gather worldwide to do what people have always done whenever they find themselves together: tell stories.

Narrative imparts a feeling of community, and community produces narratives. Narrative's ingenious achievement is above all that, in the act of speaking of a community, it creates that community as an identifiable group in the first place. This is apparent in the communications strategy of a certain company whose resource and business model is the community: Facebook. In a post from February 2017 with the heading "Building Global Community," Mark Zuckerberg was ostensibly reacting to the trauma caused by Donald Trump's presidency. In the face of Trump's isolationist politics, at the time of publication the heading seemed like a declaration of war, although the global company probably posted it out of economic and not political motivation. The boyish CEO presented the central message in a question both simple and broad in scope: "Are we all building the world we all want?"[21] The sentence's rhetorical feat lies not in its content but rather in its form, which subtly extends the reach of its pronoun. Though the speaker of the sentence's first "we all" seems to refer only to Facebook (the previous sentence is about the company's tireless work on products and updates), the second "we all" consolidates the business and its customers indiscriminately in a single group. This merger complete, the users are suddenly shifted into an active mode: global businesses and users build the world side by side, united beyond all questions of power. And isn't it true that "we" are actively involved? We all maintain our profiles and press our like buttons, don't we?

The sentences that follow could be cribbed from the management storytelling textbook: "History is the story of how we've learned to come together in ever greater numbers," the post continues, "from tribes to cities to nations. At each step, we built social infrastructure like communities, media and governments to empower us to achieve things we couldn't on our own." The previous sentences prepared "us" to think in terms of a communal we. It taps into the little fable of human civilization developing from scattered tribes to a connected global community, addressing readers collectively without further preparation. The message of this story shrinks history down to a single, huge, unified community-building process that knows no differences, inequalities, or wars, leading straight as an arrow from pre-history to our globalized present. We are currently in the final chapter of this story, and on the tip of the arrow sits a business under whose roof we can gather: Facebook. Here too the company is a burning fire around which we can warm ourselves, even in the turbulent present, assuring ourselves of our belonging.

BY THE NUMBERS

You might suspect otherwise, but actually many fans of storytelling value numbers over words. *Field Manual for a Learning Historian* is a sort of founding document of narrative management, collecting the findings and insights of the aforementioned Center for Organizational Learning at MIT. It expressly commits itself to the word: "We judge significance with words, not numbers."[22] But with the rapid spread of storytelling in the late 1990s, this dedication to the word is nonetheless disappearing. Things sound completely different when consultant Julius van de Laar of the German business-news magazine *Wirtschaftswoche* explains the ideas behind narrative managment: "Storytelling is a Trojan horse for facts and figures."[23]

Laar's statement is astonishing, not because he simply muddles the relationship between word and number but because he suggests that numbers need additional support from words. With the positivism of applied mathematics and belief in the quantifiability of life, numbers seem to currently reign supreme. They're on the side of power, and they hardly require subversive measures for legitimation or attention.

The technical-mathematical orientation of society is nothing new. By the beginning of the twentieth century, thinkers and authors such as the Austrian writer Robert Musil in *The Man without Qualities* objected that storytelling, based on anthropomorphic patterns of perception and thought, was falling by the wayside in favor of the factual, abstract rationality of technology and statistics. Since the advent of digital computers toward the end of World War II, this development has tremendously accelerated. Computer-supported simulation calculated with mathematical models, first required for the construction of the hydrogen bomb, has since become indispensable in many intellectual domains, as well as in social spheres, and especially in the field of economics. The financial crises of the past decades also attest to the fact that "computing has performatively taken on a life of its own," as well as to a general "formalization of the world."[24] Both phenomena derive in large part from the implementation of simulation models whose relationship to social reality remains hypothetical but that nonetheless has an impact on it, with far-reaching and often disastrous consequences. And yet a history of the relationship between words and numbers even in the past hundred years would prove to be both multifaceted and varied, since fascism and Stalinism can in a sense be described as the dictatorship of (propagandistic) words over numbers (as a democratic principle). Even if we know, for example, that the unemployment statistics provided by German authorities are in no way as unambiguous as the numbers suggest, that they can be easily instrumentalized,[25] and that they're often referenced manipulatively,[26] it would be misguided to deny the informative potential of numbers and statistics.

It's difficult to offset numbers with stories and vice versa, and they prove problematic as a means of social diagnosis, as is made clear by the fact that today stories can prompt negative prognoses with an authority similar to that of numbers. James Phelan is more concerned about the superior power of the story to that of the number, at least in many academic disciplines, in which the literary critic sees a "narrative imperialism"[27] at work: in psychology, pedagogy, the social and political sciences, medicine, law, theology, neurology—everywhere, people rely on storytelling. One needn't use Phelan's terminology (which implies, with "imperialism," a conscious authority and strategy behind the narrative turn): the current irony lies in the fact that the cyclical high of the numeric concept of knowledge found its mirror image in the trajectory of the narrative concept of knowledge. It has long been accepted that narrative and findings in the natural sciences aren't mutually exclusive, and even in the sciences, the insight that the organization of knowledge is largely based on narrative structures has gained traction. Narratives have gained significance as the carriers of reliable knowledge and as an affective form of communication. In the form of founding myths, they even inform entire societies, nations, and cultures, often in powerful ways. However, the role of stories can meet with distrust in the public sphere and in the media. Following the attacks on the World Trade Center, the journalist Lynn Smith reported, "Stories have become so pervasive, critics fear they have become a dangerous replacement for facts and reasoned argument.... Critics note that persuasive stories can be spun out of false memories or into propaganda. People deceive themselves with their own stories."[28]

In the United States, there is a strong sense that politics, and in particular the role of presidency, is intimately linked to the art of storytelling: "The key to American presidential leadership and the secret of presidential success is, in great measure, storytelling. From the earliest days of our republic to the present, those who wished to hold the nation's highest office have had to tell persuasive stories."[29]Particularly since the George W. Bush presidency, the role of storytelling in politics and media has been sharply scrutinized as a manipulative means for gaining and maintaining political power. Be that as it may, it is beyond any doubt that George W. Bush had advisers who briefed him well on the importance of stories. "We have a place, all of us, in a long story," George W. Bush began his 2001 inaugural address, "a story we continue but whose end we will not see." The word "story" appeared a total of ten times in the fourteen-minute speech.[30]

Storytelling's public image is also blemished in part because of the strong alliance between the Pentagon and Hollywood. For example, the Institute for Creative Technologies (ICT) at the University of Southern California, Los

Angeles, was founded in 1999 with the explicit goal of bringing researchers, the military, and Hollywood studios together to develop story lines for the film industry, as well as for military, therapeutic, and social purposes. As a result of large-scale projects like these, in the American public sphere, storytelling takes on the aspect of a "technology of communication, control, and power," as the French writer and researcher Christian Salmon puts it, calling it a means of manipulation.[31]

But if we shift our attention to the opposite pole, the power of numbers rather than stories can be equal cause for concern. The inexorable rise of computer technology is responsible; in recent years, "data evangelists"[32] have drawn attention with the keywords "big data," with which they proclaimed a "revolution that would change our lives." Big data is based on the processing of huge quantities of data and is represented exclusively with numbers. The utopia of this technology reaches its apex in "the end of theory": "Out with every theory of human behavior, from linguistics to sociology. Forget taxonomy, ontology, and psychology. Who knows why people do what they do? The point is they do it.... With enough data, the numbers speak for themselves."[33] In this vision of a technocapitalist complex with calculation-based and therefore seemingly unlimited assessment of one's environment, a "numeratocracy"[34] proclaims itself, resurrecting a sort of Platonism. Even in Plato's ideal state, numbers and their associated fields of study (mathematics and geometry) were supposed to pave the way for knowledge and truth; for Plato, it is as a mathematical discipline that even philosophy finds its highest calling.

Resistance to this Platonic numbers-based worldview has increasingly arisen of late. The implementation of a concept of knowledge based on numbers and algorithms has progressively automated processes in politics, the military, and the economy, from data collection to its evaluation, and even decision making based on that data. The elimination of democratic processes is just one fear among many raised by this trend.[35] The utopian data-lovers' false conclusions and myths have been variously exposed: data never exists merely as such, nor does it speak for itself; without questioning and hypotheses, masses of data are meaningless. In the case of algorithmic data management, algorithms function selectively and according to certain premises, and therefore they never attain objective results. Recently, pilot projects like Google's automatic photo recognition and Microsoft's Twitter-bot Tay, which used artificial intelligence algorithms, have demonstrated that algorithms are never neutral; they reproduce social attributes and inequalities, repeating racist or anti-Semitic statements. Despite all the objections and concerns, new technologies are advanced by powerful capitalist interests and dynamics but also by political ones, and the Californian ideology in particular feeds on the evangelistic belief that explicitly seeks deliverance in numbers instead of words.

At the beginning of the new millennium, words and numbers both vouch for a truth and come under suspicion of unjustified dominance. Both are also treated as means of manipulation, enlightenment, and salvation. That's why the banal yet momentous insight that the two are inextricably interdependent is so decisive—and as a storyteller, one must necessarily determine this relationship for oneself. This gives rise to two approaches to storytelling.

One position favors numbers, with words and narrative merely serving as the stirrups that help heave figures in the saddle and hold them there. "Vivid and touching tales move us more than statistics. So let's listen to some stories. Let's be moved," writes David Evans, a typical representative of this point of view: "Then let's look at some hard data and rigorous analysis before we make any big decisions."[36] Evans has no desire to forgo words, but the attributes and functions are nonetheless clearly allotted. The truth is in the numbers, but the effect is in the words: *facts tell, stories sell.*[37] We calculate with numbers, then we use words to make sure that people do what the numbers indicate.

The second position reacts against this usurpation of words by numbers. Unlike the first position, it outright refuses to locate the truth in numbers rather than in words, and it objects to the hypothesis that "the main role of stories (words) is to dress up and humanize statistics—or, at best, to generate hypotheses for future research."[38] In comparison with the first position, the second one proves to be more nuanced, and it attempts to upgrade the status of narrative in comparison with numbers. Further indications quickly accumulate that relativize and contextualize the typical objections to storytelling—for example, Ulrich, the protagonist of *The Man without Qualities*, has the misgiving that the "primitive epic" of a linear narrative generally can no longer do justice to the complexity of the present; similarly Jean-François Lyotard's thesis posits the end of grand narratives. These doubts and similar ones have been replaced by concrete analysis of the epistemological function of stories in various disciplines and contexts; for example, in understanding how stories sequence knowledge and represent it.

In general, storytelling is integrated into management functionally, so it's unsurprising that words are instrumentalized, a Trojan horse for certain aims. But the same also goes for numbers. All this strongly suggests that we should inquire into the calculation that lies behind the fusing of numbers and words. Unlike words, numbers lay claim to a certain unambiguity; evidence is supposed to be created directly from them, to the exclusion of interpretation. The aim is to create a basis for action as quickly as possible. Where numbers close off the horizon of reflection and action, stories open it up. To bring a trial to an end and force a decision, numbers are required, not stories—or, as in the scenario mentioned above, they're used as a Trojan horse, to prepare the emotional ground for numbers. This proves true even in finance, the world of numbers: "Story is the new currency in financial management." Without stories, says Dan Hendrix, president and CEO of Interface, there also isn't any capital: "You won't get someone investing time and capital with just facts. It takes more than numbers if there's a decision on the table. Attracting investors is about being a good storyteller."[39]

Unlike numbers, stories record actions; they inspire reflection, imagination, and interpretation. As abstract entities, numbers are free from all spatial and temporal fixity, whereas narrative incorporates the past and the future, anchoring itself in time and space. Good stories can also employ vagueness and ambivalence to their advantage, allowing their effects to unfold over time, once numbers have been forgotten, superseded, or transformed by a decision. Particularly in our era, when companies are confronted with high levels of economic and political uncertainty, stories can assert a decisive advantage over numbers. Horst Wildemann, a Munich-based professor and business consultant, points to the fact that companies listed on the German stock index typically plan their strategies for five- or ten-year periods, but they must often react quickly and remain capable of changing course. Managers must still formulate objectives and visions that provide milestones, but at the same time it's advisable to build in more leeway. And unlike numbers, stories can successfully give just that: They "offer orientation without confining the manager too much."[40] The differences can be further specified and elaborated, but it's clear that numbers and stories each affect a different register with different calculations.

Up to this point, the strength of the two positions should be clear: those who can make use of both numbers and stories have access to a broader range of communicative strategies. This is especially true for management, because—unlike the sciences, which seek to establish a certain form of the truth, and unlike literature, which insists that aesthetics have a value unto themselves—pragmatism reigns there. When preferences and camps nonetheless form, it demonstrates that the choice between words and numbers is shaped symbolically, and ultimately two systems and types of rationality stand in conflict with each other. In the case of words, rationality shares a strong bond with the senses. In the final analysis, two different ways of approaching the world—and therefore two forms of belief—are inevitably negotiated between words and numbers. And for a good reason: words and numbers are never neutral signs or tools. In the act of representation (or, as is now the case with numbers, simulation), they form social conditions and create realities. As cultural symbolizations they don't simply reflect reality but rather "constitute actions within their symbolic fields. They do not passively register given conditions in the manner of measuring devices; rather, and to varying degrees, they exercise transformative effects on them."[41] This indicates once again that it's all the more important to gain clarity over the structure, function, and rhetoric of words and numbers and to determine whether circumstances and concerns are presented as an element of a story or as part of an equation.

WE REALLY LOVE WORKING HERE

Being a storytelling consultant must be fascinating. In any case, they meet a great number of people and hear a great number of stories. And yet the job also has its drawbacks and is no safeguard against disillusion. "[A] number of times I go into organizations," says storytelling coach Shawn

Callahan, author of *Putting Stories to Work: Mastering Business Storytelling*, "and they talk about stories but actually they don't use stories, it is frustrating, drives me crazy."[42] The problem doesn't lie in misgivings about storytelling. On the contrary, businesses are convinced of its power—but they don't understand a thing about it. And so the same routine plays out again and again: Callahan is welcomed enthusiastically. First they want to show him what they've already put together themselves. Full of expectation, they seat him in front of a computer screen. In the clip that plays, an employee appears "sitting on a desk, speaking to the video camera. And the employee starts off by saying, hey there, this company, it is fantastic to work for, we really love working here, there is this great cafeteria, we have fantastic life plans, insurance, et cetera." Before the video is over, those in charge expect the coach to give it two euphoric thumbs up and clap them on the shoulder in approval. He then finds himself in the disagreeable position of having to explain to his clients that the fact that someone is talking doesn't mean they're telling stories. That's why "Spotting Stories" is the title of Callahan's first YouTube tutorial, in which he helps his clients identify the elements that make a story a story.

His frustrations mirror those of the theorists. As mentioned above, Roland Barthes writes of narrative: "Like life itself, it is there, international, transhistorical, transcultural." And that is precisely the problem. "Is such universality a reason for us to infer narrative's unimportance?"[43] The endless flood of stories thwarts any attempt to establish binding criteria. Since Aristotle there have been plenty of attempts at a definition, but the lack of consensus is all the more significant in light of the fact that neither narratology nor culture theory has been able to resolve it. "Storytelling ... suffers from one of the major obstacles still encountered in KM [knowledge management], namely, reaching agreement among practitioners and scholars about what storytelling is and what it is not."[44] This raises doubts about the scientific nature of storytelling, resulting in hesitation and confusion. If you cannot reliably identify the object of your scholarship, it's difficult to claim that you are applying scholarly methods. But storytelling is suited to the ideal of scientific validity, particularly since scientific studies increasingly indicate a neuronal basis for storytelling in the human brain. Thus, for many, the search for a definition represents the discipline's Achilles heel.

When oceanographer and professional storyteller Kendall Haven led a workshop at the NASA Goddard Space Flight Center in Greenbelt, Maryland, he was confronted with this dilemma. His hosts challenged him to prove his claim that narrative is the best medium for transmitting knowledge—which in this case meant better than a scientific presentation. By that point, Haven already had many years of experience to draw on. He had organized storywriting workshops for 45,000 teachers and 250,000 students and had released five audio tapes and twenty-eight books about storytelling, including three prize-winning ones: *Write Right* (1999), *Super Simple Storytelling* (2000), and *Get It Write* (2004). But the challenge to prove the effectiveness of his methods apparently touched a sore spot, and so the storyteller withdrew into seclusion.

He read more than 100,000 pages of scholarly literature; over 350 books and more than 70 qualitative and quantitative studies, which in turn referenced 1,500 articles. He combed through fifteen different disciplines: neurobiology, cognitive research, developmental psychology, clinical psychology, neurolinguistics, pedagogy, information theory, knowledge management, organizational theory, anthropology, narratology, neural net modeling, medicine, narrative therapy, and management storytelling. Persuasive proof exists for the power of storytelling, but sound definitions can't be found. In *Story Proof: The Science behind the Startling Power of Story* (2007) Haven unceremoniously turns the line of argumentation on its head: instead of linking individual stories to a general definition, he began with the results of scientific research, which stated that the human brain was evolutionarily and sociobiologically preprogrammed to think in narrative structures, and from this discovery he derived a definition of the vital ingredients for a story. The circular reasoning of his argument is one problem; the other is Haven's conclusions, which are strikingly simple, not least because his definition makes use of the term, "narration," it is supposedly trying to define: "a detailed, character-based narration of a character's struggles to overcome obstacles and reach an important goal."[45] Perhaps Haven himself distrusts this definition; that would explain the fastidious bookkeeping regarding the number of workshops and the reams of literature consulted. He wouldn't be alone in the hope of pushing through to a point at which quantity would be transformed into quality; ironically, it's a hope he shares with the data evangelists, who would like to do away with the words that Haven is trying to vindicate.

But the impulse to pin down the definition of narrative harbors other pitfalls as well. Callahan hints at this, after making his own list of four elements that constitute a story a story: time, place, character, and surprise. After providing instructions for how to reliably identify stories in everyday situations, he leaves his audience with a warning: "Let me right now tell you, it is bit of a curse as well as a benefit, because from now on, you are going to see them all over the place, you'll spotting them left, right and center." Which brings us back to Barthes and his fear that the greatest threat to the story is its ubiquity. If everything is narrative, the meaninglessness of narrative is more or less implied.

33 STORY STATEMENTS

"To be a person is to have a story to tell," says the philosopher Isak Dinesen. In the novel *Nausea*, Jean-Paul Sartre's protagonist comes to the realization, "A man is always a teller of stories," and "He sees everything that happens to him in terms of stories, and he tries to live his life as if he were recounting it." The moral philosopher Alasdair McIntyre comes to a similar conclusion from a different perspective: "Human life has a determinate form, the form of a certain kind of story." The Italian semiotician and bestselling author Umberto Eco makes things easier for himself by saying that "man is a storytelling animal by nature"; similarly, the English novelist A. S. Byatt writes, " Narration is as much a part of human nature as breath and the circulation of the blood." The management professor David M. Boje explains that "*even in organizations and businesses*," people are "natural-born storytellers." "We live in stories the way fish live in water," says the American author and speaker Daniel Taylor, "breathing them in and out." From the standpoint of moral philosophy, Charles Taylor urges, "We all *must* see our lives in story." Tham Kai Meng explains in *The Ape, the Adman, and the Astronaut: Rediscovering the Power of Storytelling* that as a marketing expert, he finds, "It is no longer just desirable to use storytelling—it is mandatory." "If you don't communicate in stories, you're not communicating at all," declare James Carville and Paul Begala in *Buck Up, Suck Up ... and Come Back When You Foul Up: 12 Winning Secrets from the War Room*. In the final pages of *The Story Factor*, Annette Simmons also raises a finger in warning: "Because you *are* a storyteller—your *life* is the most important story you will ever tell." Hans Rudolf Jost of the Change Factory in Zurich believes that "every manager should be a good storyteller." Benedikt Benenati, who introduced storytelling at Danone as a leading strategy, explains that "a good story can be told in 30 seconds in the elevator." The American screenplay writer and director Nora Ephron speaks enthusiastically of an "a-ha experience" when she discovered "that just about everything was a story"; Kendall Haven contradicts her: "Everything is *not* a story—but it could become one." The developmental psychologist Roger Schank writes, "Stories provide the framework and structure within which people order and comprehend their experiences, relate them to each other, and store them in memory." The cultural anthropologist Mary Catherine Bateson maintains that "storytelling is fundamental to the human search for meaning." Arthur Applebee comes to the conclusion that narrative "is a product of the internal workings of the mind." "Our brains are designed by evolution to develop story representations from sensory input that accurately approximate real things and experiences in the world," according to the psychologist Alison Gopnik. The philosopher Byung-Chul Han goes further, claiming summarily that "the human brain *is* a narration, a story, to which forgetting necessarily belongs"; the manager-turned-consultant Steve Denning reacts in astonishment: "When I saw how easily round-edged stories could slide into our minds, I found myself wondering whether our brains might not be hardwired to absorb stories." The neurologist Oliver Sacks thinks that each of us "constructs and lives a 'narrative' [and] this narrative is us, our identities," and the philosopher Daniel Dennett concurs: "We all try to make our material fit coherently in a good story." Jürgen Habermas qualifies that people "can develop personal identities only if they recognize that the sequences of their own actions form narratively presentable life histories; they can develop social identities only if they recognize that ... they are caught up in the narratively presentable histories of collectivities." "For all that narrative is one of our evident delights," notes Jerome Bruner, psychologist and cofounder and director of the Center for Cognitive Studies at Harvard, "it is serious business." Bob McDonald, former CEO of Procter & Gamble, also reminds us that "people will tell stories about you, whether you want them to or not. It's up to you what sort of stories will be told about you." In *Storytelling: Das Harun-al-Raschid-Prinzip: Die Kraft des Erzählens fürs Unternehmen nutzen* (Storytelling: The Harun al Rashid Principle: Using the Power of Storytelling for Businesses), Karolina Frenzel takes things one step further, writing a chapter on this insight: "Act in such a way that colleagues and customers can tell positive stories about your business." David Armstrong, author of *Managing by Storying Around*, notes in passing how to tell a story in the first place. The question is a rhetorical one: "with passion." In

Introducing Narrative Psychology, Michele Crossley quotes David Carr, noting that "for the most part it is 'normal' for us to experience such narrative coherence in the sense that, for most of us, most of the time 'things do, after all, make sense, hang together.'" Gerald Zaltman, author of *How Customers Think: Essential Insights into the Mind of the Market,* claims: "The similarity of store and story is not a coincidence"; in *Retelling a Life* the American psychologist Roy Schafer argues, "it does not matter what story is told as long as it works." Bob Johansen, fellow and onetime president of the Institute for the Future, explains that "problems can be expressed in formulas or algorithms ... but in order to understand a dilemma, a story is required," and according to Johansen, "the future is full of dilemmas." The physicist Frank Close makes a similar argument in *Lucifer's Legacy: The Meaning of Asymmetry:* "Our minds have to explain irregularities in story terms." The International Storytelling Center in Jonesborough, Tennessee, proclaimed, "Now, after years of scientific research in 17 different fields, analysts conclude that storytelling is our most powerful tool for effective communication," but the novelist Jim Harrison warns that "the answer always lies in the whole story, not just in part of it." "There will always be someone there who says, 'tell me a story' and someone there to respond," the philosopher Richard Kearney believes. "Were this not so, we would no longer be fully human."

II   AT THE EDGES OF STORYTELLING: NINE COMPARATIVE SKETCHES

OBJECTS IN THE MIRROR

Sooner or later, the gaze that forms the basis of management storytelling (along with narrative) falls back on itself. It settles on management as it is mirrored in its narrative representation. It isn't only outsiders who suspect that management is hermetically sealed in its own world, which eludes representation; insiders themselves often promulgate the notion. The higher the rank, the more decisive the affirmation of opacity typically turns out to be. In the wake of the 2008 global economic and financial crisis, a debate over the salaries of managers broke out in Germany. Josef Ackermann, then head of Deutsche Bank, let himself get carried away, proclaiming that "when others are weak, we must be strong," only to clarify: "Of course, that's spoken in the logic of a world that cannot be represented publicly. I'm aware of that."[1] It's a commonplace that managers work in an insular world that functions according to its own rules. If one nonetheless wishes to blaze a trail into the wilderness of management, there are generally two routes available: one route traverses the genealogy and history of management theory and the other treats the manager as a social phenomenon.

The latter approach has already been roughly outlined, and that should suffice to continue filling in the picture.

Some theorists maintain that the role of the manager was already known in ancient times, since civilizational achievements like the construction of the Egyptian pyramids or the Roman aqueducts would otherwise have been inconceivable.[2] The word "manager" is derived from the Latin *manus*, but it was first documented in the sixteenth century, and as a noun it first appeared in William Shakespeare's appropriately titled play, *Love's Labour's Lost*.[3] Between 1700 and 1850 the term enjoyed widespread use in Great Britain, especially in gardening and household advice books. The position of the salaried manager came into existence in the course of the nineteenth century, experiencing a slow course of professionalization beginning in the 1860s.[4] The theoretical basis of the position—with its defining commitment to "a maximum of efficiency"[5]—lies in the influence and invention of the late nineteenth century and above all the early twentieth century, when a coherent conception of management was presented for the first time at conferences and in magazines.

In the second half of the nineteenth century, industrialization led to an upheaval of the economic order, and businesses reacted accordingly. As technology revolutionized the conditions of production and the possibilities of distribution, the internationalization of trade simultaneously broadened markets. Both meant an increasing acceleration of economic processes, making the economy a trailblazer of overall societal change as a result. Before then, production and distribution processes advanced so slowly that they could be overseen by a single owner-entrepreneur—"owners managed and managers owned."[6] In 1868 the German how-to manual *Systeme von Regeln für den erfolgreichen Betrieb der Gewerbe* (Systems of Principles for the Successful Operation of a Business) still advised, "The best instruction is aloud, given by the entrepreneur himself, who is present always and everywhere, who keeps tabs on everything, and whom the employees observe as a constant example."[7] Beginning in the mid-nineteenth century, in large industrial operations such as railroad companies this model of the owner-entrepreneur was increasingly superseded by the manager model. James Beniger speaks of a "crisis of control," which caused businesses to reorganize their communications structures.[8]

No one is as closely associated with the concept of the manager at the outset of the twentieth century as Frederick Winslow Taylor (1856–1915). With his *scientific management*, Taylor undertook a radical rationalization of manufacturing processes, as well as scientification of business organization, explicitly opposing the tradition of "ordinary management,"[9] which continued to rely on oral communication and the time-tested transfer of knowledge and experience through trained employees and engineers. Although scientific management was contentious among contemporaries, and even experts hardly ever implemented it with the rigidity demanded by Taylor, its significance can hardly be overestimated. Taylor's studies were able to have such an effect only because a broad interest in optimization processes existed at the time. The era's mania for efficiency reached its peak in the teens, when it extended far beyond the technical or economic spheres, encompassing entire domains and reaching into the private sphere, where it was applied to leisure activities, courtship, and child-rearing. The criteria of rationality and efficiency, developed in the late nineteenth century in large industrial firms, were now likewise applied to the character of individuals, and the idea of self-optimization covered physical as well as intellectual work.[10] "A psychotechnical analysis of a great thinker and a champion boxer," writes Robert Musil in *The Man without Qualities*, set in 1913, "would probably show their cunning, courage, precision and technique, and the speed of their reactions in their respective fields to be the same."[11] The decisive factor is that the new measurement techniques no longer drew significant qualitative distinctions between body and mind. Thus, Musil could take things one step further and compare the genius of an intellectual or a boxer with the ability of a racehorse.

The emergence of modern management theory coincides with the birth of business consulting, an indication of their shared genesis in the new culture of efficiency. Arthur D. Little founded his consulting firm in 1886, but the concept gained popularity only after the turn of the century, when more firms, such as Harrington Emerson (1906), Gilbreth Inc. (1912), and Booz Allen Hamilton (1914), were founded. The nearly parallel development of management theory and consulting can be convincingly explained by the fact that the latter was presented as a special form of expertise with which the newcomers promised to provide orientation to executives bewildered by social and technological upheavals. As a discrete capacity, a defining feature of management expertise is that it is "at once independent and self-referential."[12] Managers and business consultants introduce new knowledge from various external domains into businesses and repurpose it, making it fit into operational structures. Such importing functions particularly well when the new knowledge suits special challenges. It "must be modular and flexible, and simultaneously follow a convincing, stable inner logic."[13]

As a result, management theory keeps its own discipline in a state of constant turbulence, and its strange flowers bloom incessantly in every bookstore's management section, with titles like *Shakespeare on Management* (1999, a bestseller), *Nietzsche für Manager* (2008), *Goethe für Manager* (2009), and even *Überholen mit 1 PS: Wie Manager von Pferden lernen* (2011, Outrun the Competition with 1 HP: How Managers Learn from Horses). Amusing as they may be, their existence is not a mere side effect, nor can it be dismissed as the consulting industry's attempt at self-definition. Rather, they illustrate managers' great reliance on content from outside their field to continually renew their insights and maxims with borrowed knowledge. That's why the Italian mountaineer Reinhold Messner and the German Benedictine padre and best-selling author Anselm Grün are both sought-after councilors for managers, in print and at workshops: both demonstrate that the knowledge acquired by business executives gains its authority not through practical relevance to business operations but through knowledge transfer and because of a structural distance. Management's openness to outside knowledge also reflects the universality of a discipline that believes it can find its guiding principles everywhere.

But the greatest accomplishment of management discourse might lie in its knack for freeing noneconomic knowledge from its existing context, gutting it of its content, and aligning it with that radically constricted set of values that capitalism in its various historical phases has legitimized and advanced. By the 1960s, the notorious keywords were increased efficiency, competitiveness, and innovation. While Taylor's practice in the early twentieth century is characterized by the creation of an anonymous, mechanistic organization system geared toward technical production processes through the elimination of individuality and personal responsibility, the emergence of the human relations movement and human resource management reversed this depersonalized orientation of organizations theory in the 1950s (with roots stretching back into the 1920s and 1930s, and with Hugo von Münsterberg, Walter Dill Scott, and Elton Mayo among the major protagonists). Beginning in the 1980s, postmodern management theory finally shifted from Fordism to post-Fordism and expanded with new models of subjectivity and organization. Individuality and personal responsibility were gradually extolled as the engine of a new concept of achievement, one that drew on human psychology and focused on questions of motivation, creativity, and the social integration of individuals into groups and businesses. "The focus no longer lay on regulating and controlling the maximum workforce in production, but rather the management of processes of innovation"; the idea of the *human motor* was superseded by the concept of *human capital*.[14] Since the 1980s, the notion of the subject as an independent, creative labor entrepreneur has been increasingly mirrored in businesses, which have redefined themselves as engaged in "cultural and affective activity" and which incorporate "employees as interpretive, emotional beings" in their organization.[15] This also explains how narrative and management storytelling found its way into businesses.

As insufficient as this abbreviated tour of twentieth-century management theory may be, the inner contradictions highlighted are a graphic illustration of its high level of mutability and its mode of operation, which nonetheless never betray its guiding principle: the objective of efficiency is upheld even as its methods are radically transformed. This point also illustrates the high level of ambivalence that has been historically inscribed in the concept of efficiency. Efficiency-improving measures can be implemented either to maintain existing conditions (organizational structures remain untouched while production processes are adapted) or to change them. In a self-referential way, efficiency always potentially covers both: it is both means *and* end, tool *and* method.[16] The important point is that it can never be shut down or come to an end.

Another approach to the manager, different from that of theory, views managers as a new social phenomenon or type. The profession of the entrepreneur as it took shape in the nineteenth century is conflicted: entrepreneurs win respect as risk-taking pioneers and the initiators of social change, and from the economist's perspective, they are as necessary in this position as they are meaningful. They are also confronted with the criticism of acting exclusively and callously in their own interest. The German Romantic writer Wilhelm Hauff (1802–1827) anticipated this image of the entrepreneur and manager at the beginning of the nineteenth century with his story "Das kalte Herz" ("The Heart of Stone"). Managers of the twentieth century have it much harder. Their stereotypes include portfolio managers, technocrats, unscrupulous restructuring specialists, and illegitimate patriarchs. Beginning in the twentieth century, as initiators of the new, entrepreneurs could benefit from the reservations people held regarding managers; in Germany in the 1990s, entrepreneurs were even exalted as politically useful "models for the future," a view that envisioned "individuals as entrepreneurs of their labor and needs."[17] Some managers themselves entertain some doubt about management. Hartmut Mehdorn, however, certainly isn't among them. With regard to his tenure as CEO of Deutsche Bahn, which was accompanied by a chorus of harsh criticisms, he cheerfully declared that "in the end ... it was all a lot of fun." Former Deutsche Telekom head Kai-Uwe Ricke, on the other hand, retrospectively celebrated leaving the managerial profession as an act of personal liberation from an externally determined existence: "I'm completely an entrepreneur again. Everything is very lively. The complete opposite of what I'd experienced before."[18]

Independent, unapproachable, and cold: empirical studies observing managers at work affirm such descriptors, even if "the ethnography of the executive suite"[19] remains underdeveloped. In *The Nature of Managerial Work* (1973) and *Managing* (2009), Henry Mintzberg relates that business heads mainly communicate, talk on the telephone, and attend meetings, rather than developing plans and strategies or, heaven forbid, philosophizing about the existence or nonexistence of the universe, as Don DeLillo portrays the multibillion-dollar finance manager and investment consultant Eric Packer doing in his novel *Cosmopolis* (2003). Midlevel managers can devote themselves to the task at hand for an average of nine minutes before they're interrupted, while windows of time lasting for a continuous half hour occur only every few days. In the often strained metaphor of the manager's task as that of a symphony member, they are neither conductor nor puppet but rather avoid making an appearance while fulfilling their function, or even being visible at all. They are occupied with details on- and offstage and must simultaneously supervise the notes of individual musicians as well as curry their sponsors' favor. As far as the actual performance goes, no task is too large or too small. In short, managers feel responsible for *everything*—completely unlike government employees, "whose unfairly derided decision-making principle is precisely whether something is 'their responsibility' or not."[20] "Some days at Chrysler," reminisced former CEO and manager Lee Iacocca, "I wouldn't have gotten up in the morning if I had known what was coming."[21] The irony of the division of labor to which managers owe their existence lies in the fact that the position reduces complexity to the same degree that it produces it.

A manager is successful to the degree to which he or she can control disorder and subdue chaos again and again without ever having to slow down and catch a breath, because they're never simply allowed to start over. For some, that's the essence of the job: "The single most striking feature of a manager's work is that it is never done."[22]

An additional factor, hardly taken into account by the empirical studies, is the competition between managers on horizontal as well as vertical axes within larger companies, as Robert Jackall observes in *Moral Mazes: The World of Corporate Managers* (1988) and as John Sculley describes in his autobiography, *Odyssey: Pepsi to Apple* (1987), when he recalls with relish the aggressive, merciless relations that the managers at PepsiCo cultivated among themselves, preparing the ground for the impossible: the long-desired victory over rival and Goliath Coca-Cola, based on percentage of market share, calculated to two decimal points. The periodic emergence of ethical breaches at companies supports those theories that assume that performance-oriented hierarchies demand a male-dominated consensus and a "yes-man culture,"[23] which is largely immune to necessary—or even performance-improving—self-correction. Under these conditions, survival rhetoric naturally belongs to the manager's self-understanding, and it is staged theatrically in the survival seminars that literally send managers alone into the wilderness.[24]

But the phenomenon of management can't be sufficiently described in this way: "Finding out what managers do is not the problem; interpreting it is."[25] This is a key insight. Managers come to the attention of outsiders only when they fail, commit flagrant transgressions, or become elite, only then stepping beyond their sphere of activity, which is as vague as it is personalized. Then they are recognized as idiosyncratic figures whose motives and actions are judged on the basis of societal moods. Rainald Goetz's novel *Johann Holtrop: Abriss einer Gesellschaft* (2012, Johann Holtrop: Overview of a Society) takes up this subject. The protagonist, Holtrop, is the CEO of an international media corporation. His figure is based on the German manager Thomas Middelhoff, who acted as chairman of the Bertelsmann media company from 1998 to 2002 and later was embroiled in bankruptcy proceedings, as well as in several legal conflicts. The novel derives its narrative contours from the elite manager's infectious mania, which the narrator consciously adopts, all while wrathfully condemning the main character's leadership as professional, moral, and personal misconduct.

Though managers usually make negative headlines as individuals, their general function is often regarded with suspicion, even if most "only" attend to administrative or operational tasks—especially from their own perspective. The managerial role as a class of its own in society first attracted interest after World War II. In *The Managerial Revolution* (1941), the political theorist John Burnham analyzes the genesis of management, then investigates its power structures. Helmut Schelsky ironically described those power structures as being created by people who "are involved in the sale of a wine enterprise here, the foreign policy of a nation there, the waging of war by various countries at one moment, the organization of a university at another."[26] Managers legitimize their power neither through their property (as bourgeois entrepreneurs do) nor through their expertise (as in Max Weber's "domination of bureaucracy"). Instead, the reorganization of businesses that put investors on one side and skilled workers on the other created a "vacancy of authority" (in Schelsky's words) that now can only be filled by managers. Nevertheless, and contrary to Burnham, in Schelsky's view managers are not united by a general authority since they neither share common interests nor have they altered property relations in such a way that would position managers as a new, independent class.

Managers accumulate this authority (however varied) through their ability to transform questions of content into questions of organization. By taking utility maximization into consideration, they gain authority over technical questions, even when they themselves know little of the technical matter at hand (which is in accord with the point made earlier that managers gain their authority through external knowledge). The knowledge and calculations specific to managers are decisive because they justify decisions to investors and boards of directors, but first and foremost they are a means of self-legitimation, since a manager's competence, freed from any technical basis, can only be assessed based on results and achievements. In addition, the manager's role "simply does away with the personal risk" traditionally associated with entrepreneurs,[27] placing managers under suspicion of dropping responsibility and risk squarely on the backs of others and prioritizing their own ends over the common good.

And so, on the whole, the deck is stacked against managers as far as their narrative representation goes. The situation is reflected in literature, whose doors generally remain closed to them, and when it does allow them entrance, managers would often do well to remain outside. Managers are beneficiaries and controllers of capital, as well as its loyal minions, and no particular knowledge—to say nothing of love—binds them to the material they oversee. As subjects, they've already squandered whatever moral credit they might have had; as authorities, they are too subordinate, and as subordinates they have too much authority to be hallowed with a literary fate. That is, the type of the manager is not well-developed enough in literature to have a particular trajectory.

But that doesn't sufficiently sum up management in its societal sphere of influence. As an idea, it has already transcended the world of business as part of the popular practice of self-optimization—as was already the case at the beginning of the twentieth century. Individuals are challenged to be independent, future-oriented risk takers, and to act in their own self-interest in all cases. They are perceived as entrepreneurs and are consciously treated as such on the job market, as well as in their personal lives and by the state. As a result, they are quickly confronted with far too much complexity. It only makes sense that they meet these demands of complexity in their personal lives analogously to a modern organization, with management techniques. It's no wonder, then, that management techniques have spread from organizations to personal life, applied equally to professional questions as to regulating emotions. But the critical point is that the two domains should be related at all.

The entrepreneurial self is thus forced to play two roles: like a personally liable business person, it must gamble with its own life. Similar to a hired manager, it must administer the available resources strategically and objectively, whether regarding education or health, with its implications for personal conduct and life in the biological sense.[28] Like a manager in a business, the individual has access to many sources of advice in this task, including books, personal coaches, and more recently personalized apps, which promise new levels of efficiency in recording and assessing processes. (Consequently, the question of power also makes an appearance in the lives of individuals; advisers and authorities on efficiency speak in its name, legitimizing it. Once again, it probably comes down to a "vacancy of authority": without fighting for power, manager-like advisers and coaches, or the programmers and producers of self-help apps and wearables, "could pick up power just lying out in the street."[29])

The system known as "management" can hardly be delineated in its entirety, but it is clear that the story of management, and the theory and figure of the manager along with it, must be told in relation to the history of neoliberalism and its development in the digital economy. The difficulty penetrating the entity in question (whether it is management theory, the manager's work and lifeworld, or the political implementation of neoliberal maxims) through narrative becomes a question of correlation, that is, how historical, social, theoretical, and normative discourses and phenomena are embodied in organizations and in the manager as an individual, intersecting and taking form within both. The "hermetically sealed" world of the manager may remain obscure, but bearing in mind all of the variation, starting with class distinctions and privilege, at some level the relationship of the individual to him- or herself and his or her environment comes to light as the flip side of the secretive manager caste. This relationship is general in scope, and not limited to *people in high places.* This bit of speculation on the interior world of managers isn't such a leap, then, if managers share fundamental preconditions with everyone else. A common vehicular warning points to the proximity of such self-reflection, as well as the pitfalls of representational relations: *Objects in the mirror are closer than they appear.*

SEPARATION ANXIETY

Generally speaking, in the domain of management storytelling, two groups form diametrically opposed poles: converts and seminarians. The converted storyteller is a manager through and through, with many years of experience in leadership positions, whose trusted methods and tools of persuasion (consisting of charts, tables, and diagrams) no longer do the job: suddenly this person hits a wall. The seminarian, on the other hand, has a liberal arts background, often with an advanced degree. Seminarians see no future for themselves in the notoriously underfunded cultural sphere but they want to put their hard-won knowledge to use. And so they decide to apply their expertise to another field, one that is just as competitive but that nonetheless promises earnings: consulting, coaching, PR.

Here, only converts are of interest to us, because they have undergone the transformation that literally turns experienced managers into novice storytellers. They also bring a new perspective on narrative as a medium and as an experience, for their conversion itself possesses a genuine narrative structure. Two aspects collapse into one in this portrait of the manager as a young author: the converts preach narrative as the privileged form of communication for organizations while drawing on the narrative of their own conversion from nonstoryteller to storyteller. In the vocabulary of ancient rhetoric, two juridical concepts merge: the eye-witness and the orator. While the former answers, bodily, for the truth, the latter produces the forcefulness of a convincing discourse. Steve Denning's story hews precisely to this arc: after a long career as a manager, he reinvented himself as an author.

Australian by birth, he worked for decades in various managerial positions for the World Bank, most recently as program director for knowledge management until 2000. Since then he's become a self-employed consultant, the

"Warren Buffett of business communication" (as Chip Heath has called him) and "one of the World's Ten Most Admired Knowledge Leaders" (per the Teleos Leadership Institute). His clients include IBM, Microsoft, McKinsey, Shell, Netflix, Lockheed Martin, McDonald's, Unilever, and Ernst & Young. Along with storytelling advice books (*Springboard: How Storytelling Ignites Action in Knowledge-Era Organizations*, 2000; *Storytelling in Organizations: How Storytelling Is Transforming 21st Century Organizations and Management*, 2004 [coauthor]; *The Leader's Guide to Storytelling: Mastering the Art and Discipline of Business Narrative*, 2005) Denning is the author of a poetry collection (*Sonnets 2000*, 2000) and a novel (*The Painter: A Novel of Pursuit*, 2000). His early career showed no indication of his later activities.

"For the first several decades of my working life, I remained firmly in the world of leadership and management," explains Denning. He followed the normal career path of a normal manager: "The organization happened to be the World Bank, but had it been any other large modern organization, the discourse would have been essentially the same—rates of return, cost-benefit analyses, risk assessment, performance targets, budgets, work programs, the bottom line, you name it."[30] Neither geography nor nationality has had any influence on his career track, which is standardized to a very high degree. Management is a global phenomenon (to which the World Bank contributes by exporting and entrenching the principles of management in numerous developing countries and poor regions, through workshops, training programs, and academies). "The forces of globalization have rendered the discourse of management and organizations thoroughly international. It's a world almost totally focused on analysis and abstraction. The virtues of sharpness, rigor, clarity, explicitness, and crispness are everywhere celebrated."

Under these conditions, a change in thinking comes as a surprise. Thus, when Denning's employer sent him to Siberia, things didn't look very promising. The geographic location reflected his new position's lack of prestige. Denning was supposed to concern himself with knowledge management, but at that point the World Bank didn't yet consider the topic to be of any importance.

The World Bank was founded in 1944 as the International Bank for Reconstruction and Development (IBRD) in reaction to the world economic crisis of 1929, with the goal of creating an institution that would work toward global economic stability. The agenda of fighting poverty through lending and making connections to world markets was first established by the World Bank president (1968–1981) and former American defense minister Robert McNamara, and it endures to this day.[31] The World Bank had become a powerful global institution during the course of the "McNamara Revolution," but by the mid-1980s it was experiencing a crisis. Wherever one looked, in Southeast Asia, India, Africa, and South America, local peoples were demonstrating against the institution, whose policies and projects had led to increased poverty, mass migration, and increased inequality in numerous countries; even in the West the bank was subject to widespread criticism. In the early 1990s, when Denning took up his new assignment, he quickly perceived the explosive power of knowledge management. Since McNamara's reorientation, the bank had invested a lot of money in research projects, amassing a globally unparalleled body of knowledge in a variety of countries and topics. But even for World Bank employees this knowledge was hardly accessible, often involving discrete pieces of information on the country in question. Organization and archiving processes were lacking, but, more important, there was no understanding that this knowledge was a seminal resource for the future, one that would ultimately find its medium in the internet.

But Denning seemed unable to promulgate his vision, despite his calculations, diagrams, and PowerPoint presentations. He was met with indifference and incomprehension. Out of desperation, he finally told a very simple story, about a single incident: a health care worker in Zambia working in a region with underdeveloped infrastructure who sought out the website for the Centers for Disease Control to find information on malaria treatment. Denning ended with a question that encapsulated his vision for the World Bank: why wasn't the bank present in this scenario, providing information for poor people in regions experiencing crisis? A more senior manager happened to be present and paying attention. A short time later Denning spoke before the World Bank president, and beginning in 1996, the institution started transforming itself into a knowledge bank, which more or less placed information management on an equal footing with finance.[32]

But that's just one facet of Denning's awakening to the importance of storytelling. The most significant aspect is that the simple story did what established management methods failed to do. "I was facing a leadership challenge for which the traditional tools of management were impotent."[33] For Denning this realization marked the beginning of a journey into the realm of storytelling. He immersed himself in the literature and visited the International Storytelling Center (ISC) in Tennessee, only to realize that the experts there had their own conceptions of storytelling that contradicted his. When he told the story about the Zambian health care worker at the ISC, he was informed that it wasn't a story at all because it lacked a sufficiently developed protagonist and a sound plot. But Denning didn't let himself be ruffled; on the contrary, he realized he'd stumbled on something new. From then on this story, whose minimalism almost keeps it from being a story at all, formed the anchor of a genre that Denning christened the "springboard story." A springboard story is intended to initiate actions by inspiring its listeners. Typical business presentations automatically refer to numbers and statistics on the matter at hand, categorically excluding visionary approaches. Narrative seeks to free itself from the status quo, making it an opportune medium for introducing something truly new. The springboard story represents just one type of story among many that can be variously utilized in different settings, as explained in Denning's numerous advice books.

Denning's path is a typical one for converts. Peter Schütt of IBM and Paul Smith of Procter & Gamble tell similar stories. At the same time, Denning's conversion stands out because it unfolded in such a systematic fashion. He ended his career as a manager, turned to self-employment, and wrote his first advice book, making his debut in the literary field. This is notable because it demonstrates a storyteller's capacity to differentiate what sort of narration is required in each context, what sort of voice will fulfill each purpose.

We might also view his publications as ambitious attempts to demonstrate his qualifications, credentialing his shift from manager to professional storyteller, just as many seminarians publish management advice books to prove their business expertise. But the novel is particularly interesting as a representative of the narrative genre. In his cosmos of storytelling, Denning assigns all narrative genres to concrete spheres of application; the novel raises the question of which function Denning allocates to art and literature.

The Painter: A Novel of Pursuit tells the story of a young painter who moves into a secluded house to dedicate himself to his painting free from distractions. A young woman accompanies him, and besides the bacon and eggs she makes for him in the morning, she hasn't a clue why he brought her along, since her only ambition is to lure him into bed. As it never occurs to him to just send the woman home, the calendric structure of the narrative develops into a record of the woman's daily attempts at seduction—of course, she has a figure "shapely enough to lead a saint astray"[34]—and the painter's resulting disgruntlement as his "productivity" and "progress" increasingly decline under her advances. For the reader, the unusual image of a sexually abstinent twenty-three year-old lightens up when the woman unexpectedly decides to become a writer. Suddenly an additional Pygmalion narrative is revealed in the novel. Now it becomes clear that the painter's abstemiousness was a reaction to his companion's previous superficiality, which threatened to corrupt his aesthetic pursuits and squandered his time: "I'm a painter, and I need *every second of my time* to capture the magnificence of nature." The young woman's decision to become a writer triggers a change of direction because it gives the artist the opportunity to instruct her in everything lacking in her character as she becomes an author. He also benefits from this relationship because she now shares his worthy interest in art. Their exchange is safeguarded through a simple rule: "I tell her that writing takes place in the mind, not in bed. ... I will propose: disinterested stimulating discourse." This pronouncement hobbles any physical desire and simultaneously indicates the direction of further developments: *disinterested stimulating discourse* paves the way for *interested stimulating intercourse*. The union at the end of the novel is accomplished under these conditions, between like-minded individuals, and is therefore a welcome one.

Obviously, the novel has some weaknesses, the worst being its blatant sexism. One thing Denning makes clear: the loftiest aspects—the sublime—are reserved for art and literature. The young woman's request for cheeseburgers from the company for which Denning would later act as a consultant is depicted as the epitome of vulgarity in the novel, which plunges the painter into the depths of a "melancholy mediocrity," from which he seeks to escape at all costs. The harder he tries to keep his aesthetic desires pure of that inane world of the masses with its consumerism and its capitalistic values, the more that world unrelentingly, surreptitiously imprints itself on his artistic practice.

Even the words with which the painter evaluates his daily work betray this contamination: "productivity," "progress," "breakthrough," "success," and all of this under his inexorable schedule, in which "every second" counts: "I paint at a breakneck speed, finding fresh insights as I go." Each morning he sets out into nature, but not to find distraction, contemplation, or liberation. His ambition is solely focused on the production and accumulation of sensory information: "When the eye sees, and the heart feels, the painter communicates meaning, and the world learns the idea of life." As a mode of representation, painting converts the observation of nature into a problem that can be approached methodically. "Despite the initial detour, it turns out to be a productive day, as one artistic problem after another is isolated, sifted into its elements, and resolved." In short, the artist is his own best manager. And so it only makes sense that he denies himself physical desire until it can feed his aesthetic production machinery.

The driving force of this aesthetic meaning-lending machine is as simple as it is thrilling: it arises from the categorical separation between the degradation of consumer capitalism and the exaltation of the world of art. By economizing objects and life itself, capitalism levels all meaning-lending processes, producing a meaning vacuum for which art is supposed to compensate. In this way the division of these spheres can engender desires that thirst for the exclusive meaning lent by art at the same rate at which capitalism eliminates it in society by turning things into goods. Because of this interdependency, the two meet in excess, capitalism with surplus capital and art with the overdetermination of meaning, revealing that the two are shackled together in the drive to generate additional value.

In this model, art and literature don't offer an escape from the logic of capitalism. In the end, you have to find solace among the seminarians: by adapting literary knowledge into organizational and management knowledge, they start where Denning's novel unwittingly leaves off. They make no bones about suggesting that it's best to discard one's habitual resistance to commodifying art to better access both spheres by way of the social and historical structures and realities that they share. That may not guarantee any escape from the dilemma, but since it's ever more difficult to designate a place outside capitalism, if you're looking for a way out, you'd probably be well advised to at least know where you're starting from.

ROYALTIES

They may be few in number, but they exist: managers who leave their careers to pursue their calling as literary writers. In a few cases they even abstain from writing crime novels, dedicating themselves to that sphere of activity whence they came—to the delight of newspaper culture sections. A few years ago the German *Manager Magazin* dedicated a feature to this species.[35] The article makes it clear that none of the renegades have any illusions about income opportunities in their new field. To make a manager's average income of 125,000 euros (as of 2012), an author who publishes a book with a retail price of €19.80 must sell at least 68,900 copies per year. In the German book market, that would be considered an extraordinary success, the magazine assures its readers and target audience (see: average income), whose relationship to sales data is no doubt such that they are unimpressed by a five-figure number.

A manager's transformation into an author apparently isn't based on financial calculations. In addition to citing dissatisfaction with their former job, managers often hark back to a passion that already afflicted them in their youth: that diffuse dream of an occupation in which one is beholden only to one's own creative will. There's hardly such a thing as too late for these newcomers to make the leap; instead, they can bank on being considered trustworthy in their new sector, for those who reliably inspire reservations are people who actually learned their craft in school, that is, graduates of the German equivalent of MFA writing programs. In comparison with the United States, these programs are still a new phenomenon in Germany. The German Institute for Literature was founded in 1995 in Leipzig. (In the GDR, it was operated from 1955 to 1990 as the Johannes R. Becher Institute.) The University of Hildesheim followed suit and started offering a major in creative writing and cultural journalism in 1999. Similar programs are on offer in Austria and Switzerland. Although the institutes are relatively small in both number and size, the flood of new releases would hardly be navigable anymore without them. Their graduates often receive a leg up in the industry with honors, a network, and know-how, and they can also count on the media's fetish for debuts, along with the literary label "*jung*," which in German means both contemporary and emerging but also simply *young*. This word awakens hopes for the new in a facile, unambiguous way, making it invaluable for the production cycles of a market that must extol the same thing, day after day, year after year. Books and texts are subject to similar pressures as textiles. For all of their objections, the media and critics are thankful that production of the new has been institutionalized in Germany for two decades, and that demands and complaints can be directed to it at a valid postal address.

The freshly forged manager-author is free of these concerns. Such authors needn't worry about the accusation that they are merely reorganizing the inventory, which may have haunted them in their old profession and which graduates of institutes must surely reckon with. By entering the literary industry, they elicit entirely different reactions. Their experience in the real world of economics is their collateral. Unlike the new, which first fulfills a functional role by perpetuating circulation in the book market, their lifeworld experience is measured normatively by critics. They embody a value, which, in an era that is concerned with evidence and the real, is among the most richly compensated (adding to the complaints that can be leveled against the "institute," because it ties young authors' evident lack of experience to aesthetic value).

In short, those who can claim insider knowledge have little to fear. In his first two business novels, former manager and popular nonfiction author Rolf Dobelli handily earned a reputation for "transferring the laws of the business world into literature." Since the economic crisis of 2008–2009, newspaper book review sections have considered Ernst-Wilhelm Händler, a former businessman turned writer and property manager, to be an expert on all matters concerning the relationship of literature to the economy, including critiques of capitalism, which Händler himself has said is hardly his cup of tea. In the cases of Dobelli and Händler, representations of the business world raise objections among the likes of *Manager Magazin*. The trifecta of greed, power, and sex in business novels leaves a bad taste in magazine editors' mouths because it's precisely the cliché with which the clueless general public pummels the industry. Since the texts in question are literature, one could assume that the editors of business magazines are poorly qualified to judge the work of people who are now first and foremost authors. Yet the authors themselves don't contradict the reproachful reading of the editors. To them, not only are the clichés true; they're practically all there is to say about the world of business. This is why Rolf Dobelli quickly grew weary of being assigned the topic and reputation of insider in his new domain, the magazine reported; from the beginning, the world of management seemed stale to him:

"All of these people leading externally determined existences, lacking their own identities! Far too little real life! How are you supposed to make a convincing story out of that?" Händler expresses similar doubts about the material. In his novel *Wenn wir sterben* (When We Die, 2002) four of the managers are women, although that evidently conflicts with the reality of German businesses. When the magazine asked why he had made this decision, the author—whose books are often described by reviewers as cool in tone— cited men's general emotional deficiency, which doesn't make for good literature. "Women can express [emotions] better. And male power rituals are so crude they can hardly be described in a literary way."

Wenn wir sterben, by far Händler's most important novel, is about three female managers who lead the Voigtländer company together and are friends. But competition in the business quickly leads to personal intrigues and power struggles, which increasingly divide the three. The women's conflict comes to an end only with the appearance of another top-level manager from the D'Wolf company (the name gives away the plot); their joint venture fails, and Voigtländer is swallowed up by the competition. Independent of its content, it is above all the novel's conceptual apparatus that makes it convincing. The idea is simple but striking, and even *Manager Magazin* accurately described the book's aesthetic method: the author doesn't emerge as the creator lending his protagonists their own, perhaps authentic, voices but rather as a capitalist and a manager who fuses the literary styles of other established authors (Elfriede

Jelinek, Rainald Goetz, Peter Handke, Robert Musil) between the covers of his own book. In this sense, he "manages" foreign narrative voices. He doesn't try to represent the so-called business world as realistically as possible. Instead, in *Wenn wir sterben*, capitalist logic itself becomes an aesthetic method.

The author's abdication of creative authority is itself nothing new; Felix Philipp Ingold has even identified a sort of elective affinity between authorship and management, which came into its own in postmodernity with the use of pastiche and collage. In the wake of cybernetics, structuralism, and systems theory, organizations as well as novels came to be understood as self-organizing, autopoietic systems, which inevitably yielded a devalorization of the manager/author as a subjective entity. From then on author-managers were no longer assigned an authoritative function, to say nothing of a creative role.[36]

On the one hand, *Wenn wir sterben* reads like the realization of Ingold's thesis; on the other hand, its actual execution (that is, how the novel converts finance capitalism into a formal concept in literary writing while integrating it thematically) is convincing and original from a literary-historical perspective.

This is all the more to Händler's credit when one compares him to other manager-writers who have taken up the classic narrator role and perpetually rely on the narrator's creative authority. In this configuration, the reader gets the creeping suspicion that the role change is supposed to compensate for what the manager's position had previously failed to deliver: ultimate control. This suspicion sets in while reading *Atomblut: Ein Wirtschaftskrimi* (Atomic Blood: A Business Thriller, 2012).

The author, Utz Claassen, is a leading German manager who started his career at the age of twenty-four with the business consulting firm McKinsey. He was promoted at age twenty-six, and subsequently became a widely known figure as the chairman of the Baden-Württemberg energy firm ENBW in 2003. His tenure at Solar Millenium AG began in 2010 but ended in conflict two months later, just after the company filed for bankruptcy. His salary demands were discussed in the media. He refrained from taking the hiring bonus of 9 million euros, but a legal battle ensued over his fixed monthly income of 100,000 euros. Claassen's creative drive went unscathed; just half a year later the then forty-eight-year-old was at work on his first novel.

In terms of language and style, the thriller could hold its own in any newspaper book review section—its formal elements include blog entries and meditations on key terms. The tried and tested maxim *write what you know*, familiar from American creative writing seminars, is fulfilled in exemplary fashion. Claassen casts a young female over-achiever and former corporate consultant with a reputation as a hatchet woman who is hired as the chairwoman of a large energy firm. Highly intelligent, she's a perfect fit for the job. On the side she maintains contact—of the amorous kind—with the art scene and with an environmental activist, who demonizes the energy company. But above all, she is driven by her unconditional urge for truth and morality. She wants to do good in her leadership position, for the company as well as for the future of society. But it's precisely in this position that she encounters a stumbling block. She realizes too late that her former mentor has been taking advantage of her the whole time as a pawn in a rigged game. In all of its simplicity, the novel's message is hardly to be refuted: in capitalism, the "bad guys" win in the end. An individual, however clever and upstanding she may be, can't accomplish anything. "If people really knew how the big game is played," the protagonist muses at the end, having resigned from her post, they would take to the streets: "There would be a revolution!"[37] Things evidently haven't progressed that far. But as to the question of who is pulling the strings in this game called capitalism, readers never find out. There are insinuations about people behind the scenes, in back rooms, maybe in China, maybe in the United States.

This question is possibly too large for a novel, and cannot be answered at the level of individual actors. But since *Atomblut* drops hints about secret intrigues and large schemes, its focus remains on those strings in spite of itself, strings the author holds in his hands and occasionally tugs with relish. Toward the end of the novel, one of the young heroine's unscrupulous opponents—they've just exchanged quotations from Shakespeare in a final clash—takes to the air one last time as a passionate paraglider, his dirty work done, only for the author to have him soar "directly into a cliff" at this lofty moment. That satisfies the reader's need for poetic justice, but it also illustrates the superiority of the classic author over the manager-author: the power to lord over a paper universe. The manager, overseen by a board of directors in the real world, is far removed from any comparable plenitude of power, and not just as the leader of a bankrupt company.

Claassen's omnipotence is certainly limited to the world of his book. In a review in the *Süddeutsche Zeitung*, he says there is interest in the film rights, but as to whether he'll write a sequel, which he could easily imagine, Claassen—once again the manager he always was—says he'll let "the market decide."[38] And so disillusion prevails once more: it seems that no one can liberate him- or herself from the invisible hand of the market.

THE LONELY CHAMBER

In the portrait of the manager as a young author, the transformation from manager to author is a marked one. But how does it work in the other direction, when authors find themselves in the position of storytelling managers?

It has become a platitude that self-management is among the requirements of modern-day conceptions of subjectivity. In this sense writers are hardly any different from nonwriters. At most, terms like "management" heighten the sullenness already present in the sacrosanct halls of literature. Particularly with respect to the work of young writers, complaints about "didacticism and a marketing mentality"[39] seem like a knee-jerk reaction among reviewers, often triggered by showy readings whose event character is an answer, and a successful one, to the media's coverage. This is affirmed by the fact that in Germany, competition-oriented events such as Berlin's Open Mike or Klagenfurt's Ingeborg Bachmann Prize are widely discussed every year—but not without the assertion on the part of the newspapers that they'd prefer not to see the spirits they've summoned. An editor commenting on the 2014 Open Mike gets closer to the heart of things: "An author who knows that he or she is not good at putting himself or herself in the limelight wouldn't even enter the competition here." That may be. After all, the participants know what awaits them. But that just means that the performative demands associated with the act of writing come first. Those who enter the ring—while journalists, literary agents, and editors crowd the stands—have acquired the necessary skills, and rightly so, because the path into the book industry is regulated this way, and not infrequently, literary careers are started here.

The question of placing authorship in the limelight isn't new. Since the turn of the twentieth century authors have increasingly discovered "the discreet forms and masks" with which they can take their "experiences among the people,"[40] as Thomas Mann declared introspectively in an informal letter from 1897. With his self-glorification, Stefan George nearly singlehandedly introduced "the modern-day German-language pop author as self-evident 'star figure' in the German literary system."[41] If in Germany in the 1990s, pop authors still managed to unite poetics and self-glorification under the premises of consumer society, and to provoke a reaction with this approach, today self-representation and the representation of others is the status quo—on social media or off, frequently with marketing measures negotiated with an agency—and even those who would rather know nothing about it must come to terms with it. In short, remoteness from the market is neither a fact of nature nor a virtue but rather an aesthetic decision that can earn its successful practitioners—such as Thomas Pynchon in the United States and Botho Strauss in Germany—more attention in the long run than provocateurs or conformists manage to glean by following the rules from the start or seeking contact with the broadest possible audience.

Authors taking center stage goes hand in hand with a "strategic personalization of the book market," "a phenomenon that has been observed for several years."[42] This is the result of the struggle for attention in a market whose extensive supply far outstrips demand. The personalization manifests in marketing strategies—along with shock strategies and emotionalization—largely executed through storytelling. Various personalization strategies that make use of narrative formats—particularly the author portrait—immediately spring to mind. More interestingly, narrative proves to be a strategy for self-promotion that touches on the core of literary work. Recursive loops of this sort emerge in most professions. The plumber who uses professional tools to fix a broken pipe in his own home, however, differs from authors who are called on to narrate their work and career history. That's because telling stories about yourself or your work isn't simply a continuation of the literary work of *storytelling*. The point at which narrative practices—storytelling here, writing there—meet brings the difference between literary storytelling and everyday storytelling to light.

General definitions of storytelling ignore these differences by naming three or seven elements that universalize it into an anthropological act. In comparison with literary narrative, storytelling has a concrete function. While the former possesses autonomy, the latter is goal-oriented. This difference might look trivial, but it can only be formulated with recourse to the idea and tradition of aesthetic autonomy, which grants literature its own sphere. Although this difference exists in theory, it is hard to discern in practice. This is particularly true for literature, when the work of art and the presentation of the author or book are conducted in the same mode of representation: by telling stories. (A comparison with other kinds of art often goes awry at this point because literature shares its medium with everyday communication; the idea of singing a piece of music criticism or painting art criticism makes the divergence clear.) The presentation of authors and books in a narrative fashion has unfolded in parallel with the phenomenon of storytelling in management, not as a result of it. In any case, by now there is no sphere in which narrative reporting is not employed. And so in the media, authors are unfailingly challenged to put their biography and their book into a tellable form.

In the best-case scenario, it falls to the writers to direct their own story; in the worst cases, they're simply accomplices to itinerant reviewers. "Portrait of the Author with a New Book" is as popular a genre in German newspapers as it is a time-tested one. The standard version opens with the journalist's sensitive introspection just before entering the author's apartment. Or the journalist observes how, like a deer striding into a clearing, the author enters the café they've agreed to meet in.

But the inverse can also be true: the author is pleased that other people enter the picture to take over the narrative communication, releasing the author from it and establishing a clear rift between the two narrative acts. This rift traverses the narrative registers, producing an echo of the "loneliness" Walter Benjamin identified as the "birthing room of the novel," in order to differentiate the premodern narrator (who was integrated into oral society) from the modern narrator, who writes from a state of isolation. The French writer and critic Maurice Blanchot spoke of the "solitude of the work," evidenced in the fact that to write is "to withdraw language from the world," a view certainly compatible with Benjamin's thesis.[43] Blanchot even deduces from it the thought that literature (in the strong sense) requires mediation, only coming into its own through interpretation. Biographical narrative isn't exactly out of place here. It typically represents the easiest way to close the divide between the two types of speech, particularly where there are few binding criteria for speaking of literature in reviews and on media platforms. Besides the *plot summary*, in this context the author biography is the telltale sign of a type of review that has largely lost touch with the confrontation and rapprochement associated with the societal task of mediating literature. This is presumably due to a general lack of interest in the relationship between literature and commentary, writing and reading, as it still prevailed in the second half of the twentieth century (for example, with the proliferation of theory). But without negotiable aesthetics every work stands for itself, and so the biographical authorial I opportunely points the way from literature to the lifeworld and back, relieving the audience of the demands of actually reading the work. The media fear leaving readers alone with a book, or even confounding their expectations. One might expect this to create leeway for authors to produce something complex, but it paradoxically coexists with consensus-driven literary production. This approach clears any hurdles out of the way in advance with its commitment to psychological, plot-driven realism.

Recognizing storytelling as a craft in its own right helps identify the narrative format for self-representation and the representation of authors. This also holds true of the transformation of self-promotion through new technologies and media; today writers make Facebook and Twitter their own, just as Thomas Mann or Stefan George did one hundred years ago with the photo portrait. And so storytelling could serve as a guide for all authors seeking "discreet forms and masks" in order to achieve what has until now apparently evaded them: to continuously narrate themselves and their work.

DEAD DOGS DON'T BITE

Rhetoric, according to Roland Barthes, is dead. Its origins reach back five centuries before Christ. By the beginning of the nineteenth century, rhetoric had largely disappeared as an applied practice, absent from philosophy starting in the Renaissance and from art and literature starting with

Romanticism. In advertising and politics, it survives in a diminished form. But its decline should come as a surprise to us. Rhetoric really could and should be at home in democracy. After all, it is oriented toward communicating to the greatest number of people, to majority decisions, and to current opinion: "... Aristotle (by his poetics, by his logic, by his rhetoric) furnishes for the entire language—narrative, discursive, and argumentative—of 'mass communications,' a complete analytical grid. ..."[44]

It's hardly any wonder that rhetoric is returning to management discourse, though methods like storytelling are explicitly dedicated to effective communication, whose success is measured from the point of view of the audience, not that of the teller or based on the story.[45] Its rhetorical heritage is also recognizable in the methodology with which advice books categorize the art of storytelling. It begins with the definition: a story has three elements, explains Paul Smith (Procter & Gamble). He turns Aristotle's definition into an acronym: "Instead of beginning, middle, end, let's call those context, action, result—CAR."[46] The choice of words is new, and the coining of a catchy mnemonic device is genuinely rhetorical. (Later, "story" is also turned into an acronym: "Subject + Treasure + Obstacle + Right lesson + whY"). This method gives some indication of the structure of the story. Various aspects are to be considered, depending on the situation. In *Squirrel Inc.: A Fable of Leadership through Storytelling*, Steve Denning organizes his chapters as follows: "How to Use Storytelling to Reveal Who You Are and Build Trust," "How to Use Storytelling to Transmit

Values," "How to Use Storytelling to Create a Future," and so on.

But method also means practice. That's why advice books tend to end with instructions for exercises. This didactic approach corresponds to the tradition of antiquity, which institutionalized rhetoric as a subject of study and standardized it by means of exercises, readings, and tests. In this sense, the new storytelling advice books have taken the place of the old lessons in rhetoric.

With some effort, the methods and means of storytelling could be translated back into the vocabulary of classical rhetoric. But that wouldn't bring to light anything new. Compared to the obsessive classification, mania for nomenclature, and endless instructions of classical rhetoric, management advice books offer a sort of emergency toolkit. Certain shifts are very evident. The focus on narration is obviously one. In ancient rhetoric, narration was a building block within speech. In storytelling, it's often the entire structure. This emphasis is accompanied by a revaluation. The argumentation of rhetorical speech is replaced by the narrative in storytelling. Rhetorical discourse is traditionally divided into four parts: *exordium*, *narratio*, *confirmatio*, and *epilog*. This division is guided by two strategic aims: to convince people and to move them. The *exordium* and *epilog* (introduction and conclusion) call on affect, while the *narratio* and *confirmatio* (story and proof) call on reason. In the *narratio*, the case is laid out. Unlike literary narration, it is "naked;" that is, it is presented without any digressions or flourishes. This is also the result of its functionality, which is completely in the service of argumentation. The *confirmatio* gathers evidence that argumentatively convinces listeners through the power of reason. In management storytelling this four-part structure and succession is boiled down to just narration. It must move its audience as well as persuade them. For managers, that means that persuasion becomes affective instead of rational.[47]

Rhetorical methods can be extended and refined through analysis in this way. Of much greater interest, however, is that storytelling doesn't acknowledge itself as rhetoric—not out of ignorance but rather because popular management expertise tends to operate neither historically nor critically, and generally suppresses its sources. Whatever it borrows is freed from its original context and presented as a "pure" tool. That's the only way that management storytelling can offer universal knowledge that can be applied to everyone and everything without distinction: people, companies, nations or economies, politics, lifeworlds. Characteristically, management literature recognizes no boundaries or fear of contact, whether the matter at hand is psychological, historical, religious, or cultural knowledge. Esoteric knowledge notoriously has an established place in management discourse.[48]

So it's no surprise that the appropriation of rhetorical knowledge is suppressed. This silencing is also symptomatic for another reason. Rhetoric contradicts the prevailing notion and practice that calls on "evidence (of facts, of ideas, of sentiments), which is self-sufficient and does without language (or imagines it does so)."[49] Since rhetoric consciously deploys language as a device, it rouses suspicions (and always has). "We consider it to be not *natural*, and as producing the impression of being done purposefully."[50] Compared with the artificiality of rhetoric, talk of evidence and factuality as "natural" language seems closer to the matter at hand, and therefore closer to the truth.

We can recognize a parallel between storytellers and writers in their dedication to storytelling, which mistrusts rhetoric. Both want to convince us that by telling their story, they are primarily carrying out an anthropologically determined act. That makes both of them romantics. "Every adult is a natural-born storyteller. You've been studying the art of storytelling ever since your parents read you bedtime stories. You already know what the structure of a good story is. All you need is to be reminded."[51] Anyone who tells stories or learns the art of storytelling, so the message goes, is following a natural calling. Tracing storytelling back to early childhood socialization, prehistoric societies, or pointing to its biology through neuroscience establishes storytelling as a nonrhetorical practice. According to rhetoric, storytelling introduces narrative as "evidence," an unmistakable sign that testifies to the speaker's "humanity" (as a pregnancy is "evidence" that a woman has had relations with a man). Infringing on the authenticity of the narrative act—and above all, emphasizing its artificiality—is among the greatest sins that storytellers can commit. It costs them their credibility.

Writers may potentially have more freedom in their simulations, but for storytellers and writers alike, their understanding of narrative arises from a shared repudiation of rhetoric. At the same time, thinking in terms of rhetoric exposes a difference in their narrative methods. Aristotelian rhetoric is divided into two separate discourses, rhetoric and poetry. Rhetoric is the art of public speech (Aristotle distinguishes three forms of rhetoric: deliberative, judicial, and ceremonial rhetoric), while poetics is the imaginative depiction of events. The idea of literature in the modern sense arose in contrast to Aristotelian rhetoric, with the merging of rhetoric and poetics. In Gorgias's concept of artistic prose, which witnesses "the advent of a decorative prose" subjected to "the rhetorical code," Barthes identifies a predecessor of modern literature as *belles lettres*.[52] Language emerges as an independent—aesthetic—object for the first time.

According to Barthes's conception, storytelling could be assigned to Aristotelian rhetoric. Their proximity is demonstrated by their oral character, which in turn is associated with brevity. Every decorative element that exists for its own sake is therefore erased: "Strip the story of unnecessary detail."[53] Maximal impoverishment of the story is the highest imperative in storytelling.

For literature, on the other hand, elaboration is essential. As fictitious speech, it originates with digression, giving rise to an idea of writing that constantly drives itself beyond itself. This becomes apparent in the Romantic and modern eras, after the loss of rhetoric signaled the breaking away of a system of rules and an ordering structure. Classic prose doesn't hesitate to repeat itself; instead, its ambition was always also to repeat what had been said according to the standards of good style, and to say it better. Modern prose, on the other hand, values originality, spontaneity, and the freedom of the subject. Emancipation leads inevitably to a loss of faith in the ability to follow the path marked by rhetoric, so literature thenceforth had to be its own justification. This becomes all the more obvious the further it pushes its elaboration, the act of writing as such increasingly determining the understanding of literature (as is the case in French with the term *écriture*). Literature becomes an endless act, which can at times lend it a quasi-transcendental status but also prevents it from achieving resolution.

To put the problem differently, in modernity, writing can no longer be grounded in anything because it is literally fathomless. In extreme cases, in its attempt to form a stable system of references, it develops between the two poles of insanity and paranoia on the one hand (suddenly everything is meaningful), and loss of reality (nothing is meaningful) on the other. However, there are many possibilities for steering clear of this dilemma: genre literature, strong plots, role models, the absolutization of the I. What all these approaches have in common is that they allow the author to move beyond the loss of an ordering framework and the problem of a system of references. What long was proclaimed as a story of progress and emancipation began to falter in the second half of the twentieth century, in some cases proving to be a complete dead end.

It is unlikely that rhetoric will make a comeback; forms of realism continue to dominate; in their demand for evidence, they refer to what is in a documentary or biographical fashion. (Magic realism does continue to enjoy some popularity in German literature, but freed from its original historical and cultural context, constituting the reverse side of this demand. It avoids the problem of forming a system of references by invoking a seemingly existing reality, typically ridding itself of the question by abandoning any epistemic interest in the relationship between language and reality.) That's precisely why reflecting on rhetoric in this context is revealing: it helps us identify a theoretical point at which storytelling and literary writing separate based on their shared dependence on rhetoric: orality and brevity in the one case, the written form and digression in the other. In storytelling, language is committed to communication and persuasion. It must amount to a statement, message, or meaning; otherwise it fails. In contrast, literature fails when it doesn't go beyond a statement, message, or meaning. It must allow language and speaking themselves to be its object and its truth. Ultimately, it may be a theoretical vanishing point, but it is significant as such: language as the medium of communication in storytelling stands in contrast to the communication of language itself in literature—and, more than an aesthetic doctrine, in the literary field this denotes an eminent political conception, if one assumes that language brings about social reality in the first place and plays a significant role in shaping it. It's worth remarking again that storytelling and literature have a shared origin in language and narration. Just as language usage acquires a political dimension, so does the relationship between literature and storytelling. Since storytelling has become commonplace in the wake of corporate storytelling, literature must be political, even against its will. We can no longer innocently claim that simply telling stories is inherently humane or good.

THINKING WITHOUT BANISTERS

The contact or even mixing of literature with all too profane things such as management and marketing typically triggers defensive reflexes, particularly among literary types. Michael Esder's study *Die enteignete Poesie* (Expropriated Poetry: How the Media, Marketing, and PR Exploit Literature) argues that media and marketing parasitically use poetic devices for their communication strategies, thereby weakening literature as a whole. Storytelling is just one phenomenon among many that make Esders uneasy. His anxiety is mainly fed by two sources: first, storytelling trivializes literature, "exploiting its forms and ways of speaking for itself," and second, a "colonialization of all areas of life" is under way in which marketing strategies appear in literary clothing, not relenting even "at the most inner and personal aspects of their consumers and clients."[54] Both sources of anxiety are bound together by a single political factor, since language represents "a highly political matter," encompassing everything from concepts and definitions to narrative conventions. By analyzing the transfer of literary forms into the economic sphere, Esders's thesis speaks to the ideas in *The New Spirit of Capitalism* (1996). In that study, the French sociologists Luc Boltanski and Ève Chiapello demonstrate how countercultural postulates were accepted and absorbed into culture in the 1960s, and particularly how the criticism posed by art was assimilated by capitalism in the following decades. Neoliberalism can thank the integration of artistic critiques and maxims (among other things) for its success, which means that countercultural demands for autonomy, self-determination, and creativity legitimated the perpetuation of capitalism, becoming guiding principles for everyone. Since then, talk of emancipation in the arts has inevitably been viewed with suspicion.

Esders leads us to imagine literature reappropriating its own territory, "reflecting on the inner, unmanageable nature of poetry." Neither authors nor literary critics would balk at this idea, but the creation of a sacred space for literature is neither as daring nor as reasonable as an approach that hazards the complex prevailing conditions. Rather than shoring itself up by securing the remaining resources (as, for example, do those who cling to a canon— or who might even wish to belong to it themselves), it takes as its starting point not the delineation and dividing up of spheres and discourses but the mutual influence of one on the other.

As a first step, we must question Esders's terminology of appropriation and dispossession. Esders speaks of modernity insofar as it conceives of art and literature as sacrosanct, drawing on the utopian promise of art as representative of a liberated subjectivity and form of life. But this idealistic conception of art also means that the legitimate control or appropriation of literature by individual writers would be just as impossible as its illegitimate appropriation by management or marketing. The territory of literature as autonomous art is determined by its historical and social context, and in this sense no one can exercise command over it at will. Proponents pose this literary sphere as absolutely autonomous; its countermodel would be a historically conceived concept gleaned from its interrelationship with economic, but also political and media-related, developments. The emergence of the novel in the sixteenth century and its development since the eighteenth century are inconceivable without the incorporation of economic and media-related conditions. In particular, the realistic novel owes its existence to the upheavals in economics and media in connection with the formation of the bourgeois class. The same goes for literature today: its relevance owes entirely to its dependence on the social and economic contexts in which writing takes place. Since the eighteenth century, literature has classically stood for a lofty realm above economics, an idealized conception that literature itself requires. But this realm apart is tainted from the outset since it attempts to reject the economic conditions attached to its genesis. As the warrantor of a liberated subjectivity and society, literature is credible only if it exposes itself to the very thing that this emancipation simultaneously impedes and annihilates. This is particularly true of contemporary capitalism, which destroys precisely that which modern literature and art traditionally seek to preserve or even to call forth in the first place: the reconciliation of the past and the future, subject and nature, society and language, work and love.

Historically, capitalism appropriates and subjugates all domains and resources to economic calculation. Neoliberalism, as it has been politically implemented since the 1980s, has decisively followed the course of "economic imperialism," seeking to extend into all areas of life, even religion, family, and love. "The horizons of economics need to be expanded," the economist Gary S. Becker programmatically explained as a representative of this school. "Economists can talk not only about the demand for cars, but also about matters such as the family, discrimination, and religion, and about prejudice, guilt, and love. Yet these areas have traditionally received little attention in economics. In that sense, it's true: I am an economic imperialist. I believe good techniques have a wide application."[55]

If we take a comparative look at modern art and literature, something very similar can be claimed about the two, but with a decisive difference. When they insist on referencing life as a whole, they do so from a powerless position. The external boundaries of art, which outline it as an independent, autonomous sphere, are simultaneously counteracted by a countermovement of dedifferentiation and the erasure of boundaries. This general expectation that art will speak to life as a whole is embedded in bourgeois art owing to its function as a social model, just as it was aggressively pursued by the historical avant-gardes.[56] In both cases it can dedicate itself to life as a whole, including the conditions of its own creation. This last point is important (not just in comparison to the economy, which is notoriously blind to its own history) because the question of their origins also means that literature and art have had to and must constantly renegotiate their spheres of activity.

It's no wonder, then, that "appropriation" has become a prominent term in the fields of art and literature. Starting with the 1917 *Fountain,* Marcel Duchamp's readymades mark the date from which an artistic practice began to transfer everyday objects and practices into aesthetic contexts, shifting and dissolving the customary borders between aesthetic and nonaesthetic things and spaces. (Today, and particularly in the American context, appropriation is most commonly discussed in terms of cultural appropriation. Here it should be understood as a general strategy of borrowing—from other cultural spheres or other artists.) Beginning with pop art and Andy Warhol in the 1950s, art was explicitly opened to the economic sphere of consumer capitalism, pointing toward the culture industry conditions of the creation of art. Ultimately, the appropriation art of the 1970s and 1980s turned again to strategies of appropriation, problematizing the status of the artist and the artwork, but also entering into a direct confrontation with the spheres of commerce, entertainment, and pop culture.

Into the 1980s, various processes of appropriation could be presented as subversive acts that destabilized the prevailing discourse or attempted to shift marginalized practices such as art into their rightful place. Since then this trust in the power of art has largely fizzled. That doesn't mean that processes of appropriation are obsolete per se, only that the boundaries and relationships are different, both less clear-cut and more complex. As such, there can also be no automatic division between the aesthetic as a good, subversive practice and the economic as a bad, perverting practice—as our current-day concern over cultural appropriation reveals.

Appropriation, even of the supposedly subversive sort that borrows from those in power rather than the oppressed, can no longer be upheld uncritically, and so using the term may ultimately steer discussions on an undesirable course. Appropriation immediately shifts the relationship to the lifeworld—and this goes for the economy as well as for literature—into a form of property relations, resources, or territorial gains (the terminology betrays the fact that this approach is deeply embedded in the capitalist way of thinking). Alternatively, and to provide contrast, this relation might be posed in terms of modes and usages, which may be primarily politically, economically, or aesthetically coded with reference to the lifeworld. Literature and economics also share a common point of origin in this sense. Minimally, a first question would be: in coming to grips with new forms and content, to what degree are its prerequisites and the situation from which literature emerges, embedded in concrete economic relations? Then one could inquire into the modalities that allow literature to have a different relationship to the lifeworld than one that is primarily economic. Or, to put it less strongly: can literature manage to demonstrate the distortions and limitations of a primarily economic relationship to the lifeworld only by referring to itself and its own use of narrative? This approach is based precisely on the insight that no separation of the economic and literary spheres can be presupposed, in the sense that the one is a discourse that addresses and structures economic relations in society as it relates to itself and what is foreign to it while the other does so for sensible relations. In this context, the phenomenon of storytelling is illuminating because it demonstrates that the economy as well as literature can tap into the lifeworld using stories, which places narrative access to the lifeworld at their shared center. Beyond this shared perspective, the various modes of narrative in the economic and literary spheres diverge, as does the degree to which each discourse makes different use of stories.

A complex relationship between storytelling and literature emerges, reflecting the correspondence between the modes and uses of narrative in storytelling and in literature, as well as their relations to the lifeworld. Two rather contradictory aspects can be identified for storytelling: power and poverty. The proof of storytelling's power in marketing and management draws on its social efficacy in the economic sphere; its poverty is expressed in the redundancy of rhetoric in commercials, company profiles, and advice books, with their obligatory positivity and pragmatism. The concrete stories in storytelling remain weak in this sense, preventing them from taking center stage with their message and its mainly unambiguous communication. Storytelling determines the meaning of the narrative; in the best cases, it becomes fully instrumental, serving as a tool that instantly provokes actions and thought. In this rubric, every reference to itself that allows the narrative to push to the foreground as narrative, shifting attention through its storyline or style to its modes, or through its goal-oriented character to how it is used, creates an unwanted diversion.

The difference between storytelling and literature is clear in this case. The emphasis on narrative mode and usage, which dwindles in storytelling, returns to preeminence in literature. Storytelling and literature can also be viewed as a chiastic structure: the social power of management storytelling intersects with the social powerlessness and marginalization of literature; the formal poverty of storytelling corresponds to the formal autonomy of literature, which forms the basis for its potential "wealth." On a formal level, this wealth can perhaps be described as complexity or overdetermination, but also as independence or self-sufficiency, the result of the formally self-contained nature of individual works. The decisive quality of this wealth lies in the fact that a life script is inherent in the literary relationship to the world, but also much more than that: a form of life. The term "form" in this construction marks a crucial continuity between literature and life. At a general level, it suggests that both derive their being by dint of a form. Literature is freed from any prescribed functional integration into society, and so it can pose the question of form in a privileged way, and inquire into form for form's sake, that is, the meaning of the form itself. This in turn makes it virulent, turning toward life, whether to reflect the current condition of society in its own form or to insist that negotiating a form is a prerequisite for considering what a good life might be, free of any predetermined objective.

Accordingly, the problem of the interrelation of economy and literature has little to do with the appropriation or exploitation of the one discourse by the other. Literature's powerlessness becomes far more distinct in view of its social irrelevance: "And so we see," Markus Metz and George Seesslen recently wrote, "that literature, insofar as it was conceived as an art in the past, hardly plays any role in the new cultural circuits of power. (At best, it is a consolation to people whose intelligence is otherwise societally not in demand.)"[57]

Along with the profitable genre segment, sophisticated literature will certainly have its niche as an ambitious or idealistic undertaking, but its powerlessness remains the crucial factor in determining which role literature will be assigned in society, and what significance it can claim for itself. Just as storytelling's power accrues from social and cultural structures, the very same factors determine the powerlessness of literature. Neither storytelling nor literature is a matter of individuals, however successful a person with a large audience or a work may be. That also means that the heightened tone of management literature that has prevailed in recent years can hardly be countered by critique or analysis, particularly by literature with its marginalized position.

There is hope for the role of literature if the real and symbolic power of management discourse and its efficacy—which storytelling draws from narrative, a sphere shared with literature—could be diverted. When literature and storytelling come into conflict, attention and power would increasingly accrue to literature, its narrative, and the way it lends form to life. From this perspective, literature must simply lead the way forward. It must bank on its contact with storytelling to strengthen and not weaken it; its sphere of influence can grow through the mixing of domains, rather than being reduced. And so, from a literary perspective, storytelling is to be welcomed, not condemned. Independent of its form or quality, the practice of storytelling demonstrates that we are reliant on structuring our lifeworld in a narrative way, and that our relationship to reality is enriched in a sensible fashion and given new structure. And wherever stories are told, literature can make an appearance. This is because economics and literature, storytelling and literary narrative, all reflect a shared lifeworld, making the condition of social relations visible and negotiating them. When the focal points and the boundaries shift, so too do the stories. And so storytelling keeps alive the hope that the social irrelevance of literature is not yet so advanced as the media and public opinion might suggest.

WIZARDS AND CASTLES

The relationship of storytelling and literature to power can also be viewed from another angle: aren't we being hoodwinked by storytellers when we believe their claims of efficacy, or take them too seriously? Ironically, this suspicion is also raised about voices that warn of negative influences, in an effort to demystify storytelling as a rhetorical strategy, as well as against positions like the one represented here, which assumes that storytelling is largely resistant to conventional criticism and therefore demands different approaches.

Typically, talk of effectiveness falls short because it can hardly be verified. That is also precisely its advantage. It can circulate as a claim without risking being discredited. Ultimately, the topos of effectiveness is less critical along the axis of truth and fraud than in the domain of belief—or even magic. In any case, these phenomena quickly undermine typical cause-effect correlations. Instead (performative) speech acts come into play, which confine certain forces or set them free. That's why enlightening gestures aimed at simply exposing or demystifying the matter easily fall short of their target.

In general, the Enlightenment sought to drive every type of superstition and magic out of reason. As Theodor W. Adorno and Max Horkheimer argue in *Dialectic of Enlightenment*, this process doesn't occur in a one-dimensional way, but rather takes a winding course. The attempt to break through mythical worldviews by means of instrumental reason founders again and again, generating new myths. In a certain sense, enlightenment is based on anything but reason. Left to its own devices, it would ultimately turn against itself; as Adorno and Horkheimer emphasize, instrumental reason is never free from violence and can generate self-destructive energies. Thus it may not even be desirable to bring an end to magic through enlightenment and reason.

Enlightenment is also dependent on magic for another reason: it must call on and confirm magic in order to legitimate itself. Christian Salmon's critical examination of this phenomenon demonstrates that this logic also applies to storytelling. The subtitle of his study, *Storytelling: Bewitching the Modern Mind*, points to the fact that the author must first reinforce the magic of storytelling, which he tries to unveil as manipulative rhetoric. But in doing so he perpetuates the very thing he is trying to banish from the world: belief in the power and magic of storytelling.

In comparison to critics, storytellers hold a much stronger position. They can simply let storytelling's reputation work for them. Seldom must they demonstrate the effects of their art. But even where the effects of their stories are under suspicion, they can still identify themselves as storytellers (and the example of individual, concrete stories), referencing the medium of storytelling (and narrative itself) appointing themselves to the role of messenger. They are simply at the service of the story, carrying the torch of its magic, not igniting it in the first place.

Anyone can simply slip into the role of a storyteller and enchant customers just as children are enchanted by fairy tales. Magicians and children are complementary figures. We've already discussed how storytelling has its roots in childhood, and storytellers therefore have a close relationship to children. Anyone who wants to be a storyteller need only become a child again. Ultimately, the art of storytelling lies in its simplicity, in once again entering that realm of childlike innocence in which we allow ourselves to be enchanted by fairy tales, and to enchant others with childlike fantasies—just as some great modern artists supposedly worked their entire lives to become the children that they presumably once had been.

Thus, when Steve Clayton was asked how he would tell the story of Microsoft as a children's story, he was unfazed. The request is in no way an impertinence; it does not lower the storyteller and company to the level of a children's story, undersell them, or make them seem ridiculous. On the contrary, the request for the children's story sets the stage on which Clayton can prove his storytelling artistry. For the magnitude of narrative effort is inversely proportional to the reduction in complexity. How does the fairy tale called *Microsoft* go?

Steve Clayton: "If Microsoft was a children's story, it would be about a collection of wizards who live inside a castle. They'd invent amazing things that would be the source of progress to many people, but nobody would know where these magical inventions came from."

It would be useless to unmask this story or object to it as an unacceptable simplification that amounts to infantilization. The if-then formulation calls on the imagination and the willing suspension of disbelief familiar from literature. It's also unclear whether the narrator in this example is a wizard himself or just a messenger bringing tidings into the world from the programmers and engineers, the real wizards in the enchanted Microsoft castle. You can reject this communication strategy and refuse to allow yourself to be placed in the position of a child. But that neither negates its claim to validity, nor is its power in any way diminished. It simply requires others who are willing to be enchanted—or even just our belief that these others exist.

The dynamic in effect here works in much the same way that a game works. A game is guided by rules and produces its meaning and truth only in use. The players can think what they like of the rules as long as they accept them in some form, or believe in the game's rule-establishing power. Even bedazzlement and fraud need not discredit the game; they may even be the conditions for its possibility. The players consent to arbitrary rules, which then are obligatory. In this sense, the game is based on a mutually generated illusion: it "is the condition for the functioning of a game of which it is also, at least partially, the product."[58] The fact that the game is illusory, however, tells us nothing about its status as reality or its power to effect change, which it first produces through implementation. In this sense the game can be applied to all social domains and processes. It is in no way an accident that game theory emerged from economics and is rooted in the world of finance; however, games (in the sense of rule-determined structures) are also "played" in politics and in courtrooms. The conditions for accessing power and social and cultural capital, as well as their distribution, are similarly determined by the rules of a game. The attitude of individuals toward the rules is extraneous. "Anyone who desires social participation must 'play the game,'" as Albrecht Koschorke has written, "in the sense of the Latin *inludere*, from which the word illusion is derived, and which denotes the willingness to believe in the game that is currently being conducted and in the importance of its rules."[59]

But this arrangement doesn't even require the belief of individuals; they can doubt—as long as they believe that the others believe in the game. This diminished form of belief is sufficient for the game to function or the magic to have its desired effect.

To return to storytelling, this is not to discredit analysis and criticism. Their effectiveness is very doubtful, however, particularly when it comes to diminishing storytelling's claims to validity, in its conscious and exaggerated naïveté and its ability to present itself as children's stories and fairy tales. Children's stories glorify naïveté from the outset with their structure of communication. Childlike magic and enlightened demystifying proceed along different affective and cognitive registers, passing each other by or even harmoniously coexisting. If children's stories manage to make themselves immune to criticism in this way, another strategy might consist in meeting magic with countermagic (which doesn't mean that you have to meet your opponent eye to eye). Instead of driving out magic or breaking its spell, it is diverted in order to benefit from its power. This lesson can also be stated more prosaically with a formulation by the economist Nassim Taleb: "You need a story to displace a story."[60]

TOWARD A NEW THEORY OF EFFECTIVENESS

In a fictive letter dated December 10, 1898, the French writer André Gide praised the late translation of Nietzsche's work into French, long after the reputation of the German philosopher had been established in France: "One might almost say that Nietzsche's influence is more important than his work, that his work is only one of influence."[61] Gide's comment suggests that the effect of a work surpasses the work and exists independent of it, but also that the work is based mainly on its effect and is ultimately uncoupled from its substance. For all of his irony, Gide demonstrates a literary self-conception that is actually in agreement with Nietzsche's philosophy. While theories of effect generally begin with the work and inquire into means and ways that yield this or that effect, Nietzsche inverts the relationship: the effect makes the work. This approach found emphatic affirmation in the second half of the twentieth century, particularly in French philosophy.[62]

Contemporary critics and writers still find this conception strange; for them, the work is what counts. Nietzsche's attitude is much more intuitive for storytelling. To the degree that storytelling is based on literature—and this is by and large the case—it adapts literary history in a Nietzschean way as the history of efficacy and swears by its own world-changing power. Storyteller Gianluigi Ricuperati claimed in an interview with Steve Clayton that storytellers "do what great fiction storytellers always do—change the world by telling a transforming parable."[63]

Because storytelling mainly conceives of narrative in a goal-oriented fashion, it is primarily interested in the forces that it produces, not just in life but also in literature. The advice books achieve this by suggesting a specific type of story for each setting. Or they invent genres themselves, as Steve Denning did with the "springboard" or the "grapevine" story, which are determined by their function. Belief in effect is thus wholeheartedly inculcated in storytelling. In response to the question of whether his work as chief storyteller at Microsoft changed public opinion of the business, Steve Clayton answered, "In many small ways, yes. There are lots of other contributory factors, like innovative products, but all these details come together to slowly shift perception. It doesn't happen overnight, as it's like turning the proverbial tanker—it happens slowly, slowly, slowly. And then all at once." The company has 100,000 employees, but Clayton clearly has no doubt that he and his team have an impact on its course—including radical maneuvers. The role of the pioneer, insofar as effect-oriented storytelling allows it to be conceived and implemented, goes not to Microsoft but rather to Coca-Cola.

A theory of effect lies at the center of Coca-Cola's "Content 2020" marketing strategy, which aspires to move from *one-way storytelling* to *dynamic storytelling* by identifying five "capability areas" to achieve its goal, five modes that delineate various storytelling formats. This little typology is the incubation chamber for a rhetorical marketing strategy: first comes the serial story, then the multilayered story, then the sharable story; fourth is the story of immersion and discovery, and the fifth mode concerns mobilization and active participation on the part of listeners by means of the narration. These mode types (which aren't described in more detail) all have in common that they describe narrative strategies that integrate the listener and ensure that the story will be continuously passed on. These narrative formats are less focused on ending with a certain message or truth than with generating further stories. They can be continuations, variations, or adaptations, as long as they create new opportunities for reaching new circles of listeners or users, or simply extend the story in time in order to maintain a presence.

The medium of the internet may be a new one, but the theoretical calculations about narration can hardly be described as such. Instead, the figure of the oral storyteller crops up once again in the heart of the digital economy, just as Walter Benjamin conceived of it. Collecting stories and passing them on imitates the actions of oral storytelling, turning listeners into new storytellers; both of these actions are central to Benjamin's idea of oral storytelling as a genuinely collective form of communication. This corresponds to the company-as-platform, in which the company sees itself as a collecting point for stories, but also with the shift from *one-way storytelling*, which is based on a bipolar structure of sender and receiver, to *dynamic storytelling*, which is freed from the entity of the storyteller to distribute itself among as many channels and hubs as possible. What's more, the methods of use of storytelling are similar; both Benjamin and Coca-Cola emphasize practice. Thus Benjamin assigns storytelling a primarily community-building function. It brings people together and allows experiences and knowledge to be transmitted. It doesn't really matter that Benjamin's conception of the oral storyteller is anachronistic; when he developed his ideas at the beginning of the twentieth century, traditional oral societal structures were already long a thing of the past. At most the anachronism is noteworthy because it reminds us that Benjamin's narrator does not suddenly return in the internet age, bringing along a promise once bound to orality. Storytelling's directness, which once could be ascribed to an interaction grounded in presence, has entered the new technology, stoking high expectations for the internet and social media as means of communication. "Some people still think that communicating through technology is somewhat faceless compared with speaking in person. I disagree," explains Steve Clayton. "What technology does allow us to do is to be more present, in more places, in more ways."[64]

For Nietzsche, the path of effectiveness had to pass through the needle's eye of style. Unencumbered by any sense of modesty, he named himself the greatest stylist of his time, claiming that, after Luther and Goethe, with his *Thus Spoke Zarathustra* the German language had finally come into its own. With its guidelines, the cola company struck out on a different path. Neither work nor style but rather the ideal of the oral story marked the way to effectiveness. At the same time, new technologies caused conceptions of orality and voice to change into something we might call narrative format. The company's strategies speak to a transformation of storytelling under digital conditions.

The return of storytelling—in digital media or with companies like Coca-Cola or Microsoft—is in no way self-evident. In *The Language of the New Media*, Lev Manovich refers to databases and narratives as "natural enemies" and asks himself why databases hadn't put an end to narrative in the field of new media.[65] The database is closely tied to the way computers function. Databases save and structure data and, along with algorithms, are the basis for programming computers. Narrative, on the other hand, displays no particular relationship to computers. If Manovich deduces an end to narrative and speculates as to whether databases will replace narratives as the dominant form of modern cultural expression, his argumentation resembles Benjamin's thesis about the downfall of the story in the information age. Both posit a new approach to information and new technologies of data management in a one-way causal relationship with storytelling. It's true the new technologies change storytelling in fundamental ways. But thinking in terms of one-way processes and polar oppositions often leads us astray. A better description would be a multilayered web that binds together the old and new media. And in general, we could very well speculate about the new power of storytelling through digital media rather than its endangerment. In any case, we should take notice when companies like Coca-Cola and Microsoft move narrative to the center of their communications strategies. Certainly it's no coincidence that, among all the available forms of communication, this traditional medium is particularly suitable. It seems that storytelling is required to gain attention and influence in the age of new media. As in the case of Tim Cook and Apple, it suggests that the role the digital economy will play in the future also largely depends on the stories that are told about it and that we tell about it. This is precisely how many storytellers understand their role, for example when Gianluigi Ricuperati introduces Clayton to readers: Clayton "is living proof that big corporations and the future of capitalism itself are going to welcome the arrival of narrative designers: those able to choose the best words, the storylines that set things right."[66]

Since literature currently has little to say about the relevance of its own discipline, and since digital media provokes unease among their practitioners, a new avant-garde seems to be gathering among management consultants, marketing experts, and storytellers in global companies, who are inquiring into storytelling under global and digital conditions. "The point is that the company, in its most cutting-edge incarnation, has become the arena in which narratives and fictions, metaphors and metonymies and symbol networks at their most dynamic and incisive are being generated, worked through and transformed." That's Tom McCarthy's diagnosis. He discusses the topic in his most recent novel, *Satin Island*. The novel consists of an anthropologist's "field notes," from which he's supposed to write a "great report" for the company that employs him. With his narrator's project, McCarthy poses the basic question of whether it is possible to describe the present, but also whether literary *writing* is possible in the emphatic sense. The challenge for McCarthy is of an epistemic and poetic nature, but it is also rooted in contemporary conditions of capitalism and media. The function of recording life has been taken over by new technologies and programs, which record data beyond the abilities and capacities of literary craft. On the other hand, highly effective new forms of storytelling have been developed by global companies, so that literature threatens to become stranded between these two poles. "While 'official' fiction has retreated into comforting nostalgia about kings and queens, or supposed tales of the contemporary rendered in an equally nostalgic mode of unexamined realism, it is funky architecture firms, digital media companies and brand consultancies that have assumed the mantle of the cultural avant garde."[67] Accordingly, in *Satin Island*, the company's sphere of activity is summed up: "We dealt ... in narratives."[68]. Belief in the power of narrative was unabated when it was introduced to the corporate world in the 1990s to "lend it a soul," as Gilles Deleuze has written, "which is surely the most terrifying news in the world."[69] At the start of the third millennium, the new media have fueled this belief again, and the most terrifying news in the world has become common sense. And so with its "Content 2020" strategy, Coca-Cola wants nothing less than to double its turnover within seven years, as the leader in a global market that is largely saturated. Their means: narrative; the way: new narrative formats.

THE LION

Back then I was working together with an excellent copywriter. At the ceremony, we were presented with some awards. Tom received one, a Golden Lion, and when you win, well, you celebrate. After the ceremony we went to the MSM party. That was when they still threw it in Palm Beach. But as you might guess, golden lions aren't exactly light, especially when you have to carry them around the whole evening. Tom had been dragging his golden lion around the party for a while, and so he thought, okay, everyone has seen me with my lion and they know it's mine. And so he decides to get rid of the lion and finally have his hands free. He wants a drink in each hand, not just one. It dawns on Tom to bury the golden lion on the beach. It's a calm, clear night. He marks the spot with a straw from his drink. —How do I put it? We were several thousand kilometers away from home, on a beach. It was the middle of the night, Tom had already been partying hard, and now he was sticking this red straw into the sand where he'd buried his golden lion ... so far so good. Tom goes back, dances, the party was ace, we all had so much fun. At some point he comes back to the bar. I happened to be standing there with a couple of friends, Nick and Yuan, a few other people from the team, Lilian, and of course we asked him right away: Tom, where's your golden lion? And so he tells us that he buried it out on the beach, and so we, well. ... We couldn't believe it, we grabbed him right away and pulled him together down to the beach. The sand had lost the warmth of the day and Tom had some trouble orienting himself because the lounge chairs ... the whole arrangement of the chairs was suddenly different, he tried to explain to us. A few strands of hair stuck to the sweat on his forehead. His voice was hoarse, he'd been talking all night, singing, shouting, and of course there was no red straw to be seen far and wide. And he kept looking for tracks in the sand. If he had been there, there must be tracks, his, he tried to remember, went through everything in his head step by step, once, twice, but without success, without finding anything. And of course we could hardly pull ourselves together we were laughing so hard at Tom wandering around drunk and totally freaking out. What you have to know is that we were working together with Nokia, and so Yuan and I had our first N90–6 phones. Back then that was a pretty big deal, they'd just come onto the market, with a video function, and so we started filming him with our phones, Tom out there on the beach digging for his lion.

I was back home on the phone with him a few days, or maybe it was a few weeks later, and he told me he was really upset about his lion and so on and basically he really wanted it back. So I decided just for kicks to make a little clip out of the material we'd spontaneously filmed that night. And, well, it was basically intended as a sort of reward video—anyone who happened to find the trophy could contact us. We would give them money and get the lion back, that was the deal. If I remember right, first we only put the video on our homepage. In any case it turned into a viral thing really fast, two hundred thousand clicks in the first days, something like that, and absolutely everyone in the industry—*everyone*, worldwide, knew about Tom's golden lion and asked what had happened with it. It was a big deal, we were totally surprised, totally bowled over. We still haven't found the lion.

Acknowledgments

I first got started on the topic of storytelling with a piece commissioned by the literary magazine *metamorphosen*. Matthes & Seitz Berlin encouraged me to expand on the topic. Morten Paul and Kathrin Schönegg helped shape the manuscript. Special thanks go to Amanda DeMarco, who further honed and tightened the book with her translation.

Previous versions and parts of the essay have appeared as "Mach es anders: Erzähl! Eine Handreichung aus dem Storytelling-Management," *metamorphosen* 36 (2014): 6–14; "Porträt des Managers," *Merkur* 794 (July 2015): 79–85; and "33 Story-Statements," in *Das Denkzeichen: Vollelektronische für Zeitgeist und Realitätszuwachs* 85 (August 31, 2015), http://www.volksbuehne-berlin.de/deutsch/denkzeichen/denkzeichen_2015_16.

Notes

AT THE HEART OF STORYTELLING

1. David Barry, Catherine D. Cramton, and Stephen J. Carrol, "Navigating the Garbage Can: How Agendas Help Managers Cope with Job Realities," *Academy of Management Executives* 11, no. 2 (1997): 26–42, 27.

2. Karin Thier, *Storytelling: Eine narrative Managementmethode* (Heidelberg 2006), x. The following quotations are from the same page; see 42ff.

3. Walter Benjamin, "The Storyteller," in *Illuminations: Essays and Reflections*, ed. Hannah Arendt, updated ed. (New York: Harcourt Brace Jovanovich, 2007), 83–110.

4. In the first paragraph of my interpretation of Andersen's fairy tale, I reference the ideas and readings of Thomas Frank et al., *Des Kaisers neue Kleider: Über das Imaginäre politischer Herrschaft* (Frankfurt am Main: Fischer Verlag, 2002).

5. Luc Boltanski and Arnaud Esquerre, "The Economic Life of Things: Commodities, Collectibles, Assets," *New Left Review* 98 (2016): 31–54, 53.

6. This anecdote and its context are taken from Walter Isaacson, *Steve Jobs* (New York: Simon & Schuster, 2011), and John Sculley and John A. Byrne, *Odyssey: Pepsi to Apple*, updated ed. (New York: Fontana Press, 1989).

7. Isaacson, *Steve Jobs,* 236.

8. Sculley and Byrne, *Odyssey,* ix.

9. Sculley and Byrne, *Odyssey,* 90.

10. Steve Jobs, "You've Got to Find What You Love," speech at Stanford University, 2005, YouTube video, October 5, 2011, https://www.youtube.com/watch?v=3Nvjdrq6OLw.

11. Art Kleiner und George Roth, *Field Manual for a Learning Historian, Version 4.0*, October 28, 1996, 18, https://c.ymcdn.com/sites/www.solonline.org/resource/resmgr/docs/fieldmanualpreview.pdf.

12. His talk is available as a video at http://www.youtube.com/watch?v=wJ3QciZxuMA and as a PDF at http://www.daimler.com/dokumente/investoren/hauptversammlung/daimler-ir-hv-redezetsche-2014.pdf. The quotations and information cited were taken from these two sources.

13. Henry Mintzberg, *The Nature of Managerial Work* (New York: Longman, 1973), 35.

14. Paul Smith, *Lead with a Story: A Guide to Crafting Business Narratives that Captivate, Convince, and Inspire* (New York: McGraw-Hill Education, 2012), 28.

15. Rosabeth Moss Kanter, *Evolve! Succeeding in the Digital Culture of Tomorrow* (Boston: Harvard Business Review Press, 2001), 265.

16. Thier, *Storytelling*, 13.

17. Albrecht Koschorke, *Wahrheit und Erfindung: Grundzüge einer Allgemeinen Erzähltheorie* (Frankfurt am Main: Fischer Verlag, 2012), 22.

18. Thier, *Storytelling*, 13.

19. Tham Khai Meng has spoken about storytelling on several occasions. The passage quoted comes from a YouTube clip, "How to Win a Film Lion with Tham Khai Meng," in which he explains what makes a prizewinning advertising spot as a juror of the Cannes Lions International Festival of Creativity. Available at https://www.youtube.com/watch?v=7cY1aKtutms.

20. "Coca-Cola Content 2020 Initiative Strategy Video: Part I and II," YouTube video, July 7, 2012, http://www.youtube.com/watch?v=G1P3r2EsAos.

21. Mark Zuckerberg, "Building Global Community," Facebook post, February 16, 2017, https://www.facebook.com/notes/mark-zuckerberg/building-global-community/10103508221158471.

22. Kleiner and Roth, *Field Manual for a Learning Historian*," 22.

23. Kirstin Schmidt, "Geschichten erzählen—für Kunden und Mitarbeiter," interview, *Wirtschaftswoche*, April 25, 2014.

24. Jens Schröter, "Simulation (Marx und Heidegger)," in *Media Marx: Ein Handbuch* , ed. Jens Schröter, Gregor Schwering, and Urs Stähli (Bielefeld: Transcript Verlag, 2006), 303–314, 308.

25. See Claus Peter Ortlieb, "Die Zahlen als Medium und Fetisch," in Schröter et al., eds., *Media Marx*, 151–165.

26. See Stefanie Kara, "Lügen nach Zahlen," *Die Zeit* 18 (April 26, 2017).

27. Quoted in Matti Hyvärinen, "Towards a Conceptual History of Narrative," in *Collegium: Studies across Disciplines in the Humanities and Social Sciences* 1 (2006): 20–41, 20, https://helda.helsinki.fi/bitstream/handle/10138/25742/001_04_hyvarinen.pdf?sequence=1.

28. Lynn Smith, "Not the Same Old Story," *Los Angeles Times*, November 11, 2001, http://articles.latimes.com/2001/nov/11/news/cl-2758.

29. Evan Cornog, *The Power and the Story: How the Crafted Presidential Narrative Has Determined Political Success from George Washington to George W. Bush* (New York: Penguin, 2004), 1.

30. George W. Bush, "Inaugural Address," January 20, 2001, http://www.presidency.ucsb.edu/ws/?pid=25853.

31. Christian Salmon, *Storytelling: Bewitching the Modern Mind* (London: Verso, 2010), 6. Salmon's main focus is on America.

32. Kate Crawford, "Think Again: Big Data. Why the Rise of Machines Isn't All It's Cracked Up to Be," *Foreign Policy*, May 10, 2013, http://foreignpolicy.com/2013/05/10/think-again -big-data.

33. Chris Anderson, "The End of Theory: The Data Deluge Makes the Scientific Method Obsolete," *Wired*, June 23, 2008, http://www.wired.com/science/discoveries/magazine/16-07/pb_theory.

34. Roberto Simanowski, *Data Love*, trans. Brigitte Pichon, Dorian Rudnytsky, and John Cayley (New York: Columbia University Press, 2014), 70.

35. See Dirk Helbig et al., "Das Digital-Manifest: Digitale Demokratie statt Datendiktatur," *Spektrum der Wissenschaft*, January 2016, http://www.spektrum.de/news/wie-algorithmen -und-big-data-unsere-zukunft-bestimmen/1375933.

36. David Evans, "The Danger of Stories," *People, Spaces, Deliberation* (blog), World Bank, December 18, 2013, http://blogs .worldbank.org/publicsphere/danger-stories.

37. James Carville and Paul Begala, *Buck Up, Suck Up ... and Come Back When You Foul Up: 12 Winning Secrets from the War Room* (New York: Simon & Schuster, 2002), 108.

38. Heather Lanthorn, "Anecdotes and Simple Observations Are Dangerous; Words and Narratives Are Not," *People, Spaces, Deliberation* (blog), World Bank, January 23, 2014, http:// blogs.worldbank.org/publicsphere/anecdotes-and-simple -observations-are-dangerous-words-and-narratives-are -not.

39. Quoted in Alicia Korten and Karen Dietz, "Who Said Money Is Everything? Story Is the New Currency in Financial Management," in *Wake Me Up When the Data Is Over*, ed. Lori Silverman (San Francisco: Wiley, 2006), 78–92, 78.

40. Horst Wildemann, "Weniger Kontrolle bringt's," *Die Zeit*, April 12, 2017, 16.

41. Albrecht Koschorke, *On Hitler's Mein Kampf: The Poetics of National Socialism* (Cambridge, MA: MIT Press, 2017), 3–4.

42. Shawn Callahan, "Storytelling Tips for Leaders: No. 1. Spotting Stories," YouTube, January 7, 2013, http://www.youtube.com/watch?v=EkvW9leJq2E.

43. Roland Barthes, *The Semiotic Challenge*, trans. Richard Howard (Berkeley: University of California Press, 1994), 95–96.

44. Kimiz Dalkir and Erica Wiseman, "Organizational Storytelling and Knowledge Management: A Survey," *Storytelling, Self, Society: An Interdisciplinary Journal of Storytelling Studies* 1 (January 2004): 57–73, 53.

45. Kendall Haven, *Story Proof: The Science behind the Startling Power of Story* (Westport, CT: Libraries Unlimited, 2007), 79.

AT THE EDGES OF STORYTELLING

1. Quoted in Barbara Nolte and Jan Heidtmann, *Die da oben: Innenansichten aus deutschen Chefetagen* (Frankfurt am Main: Suhrkamp, 2009), 8. The idea of the world of management as a "hermetically sealed" world also comes from the foreword, p. 8.

2. See, for example, Claude S. George, *The History of Management Thought* (Englewood Cliffs, NJ: Prentice Hall, 1972), 1–27.

3. See Joachim Ritter et al., eds., *Historisches Wörterbuch der Philosophie*, vol. 5, *L-MN* (Basel: Schwabe Verlag, 1980), 709.

4. See Thomas K. McCraw, ed., *Creating Modern Capitalism: How Entrepreneurs, Companies, and Countries Triumphed in Three Industrial Revolutions* (Cambridge, MA: Harvard University Press, 1999), 14.

5. Hano Johannsen and G. Terry Page, *International Dictionary of Management* (London: Kogan Page, 1995), 186.

6. Alfred Chandler, *The Visible Hand: The Managerial Revolution in American Business* (Cambridge, MA: Harvard University Press, 1977), 9.

7. Quoted in Jürgen Kocka, "Management in der Industrialisierung: Die Entstehung und Entwicklung des klassischen Musters," *Zeitschrift für Unternehmensgeschichte* 44, no. 2 (1999): 135–149, 138.

8. See James R. Beniger, *The Control Revolution* (Cambridge, MA: Harvard University Press, 1986).

9. Frederick W. Taylor, *Principles of Scientific Management* (New York: Harper & Brothers, 1911), 30.

10. See Thomas Steinfeld, *Ich will, Ich kann: Moderne und Selbstoptimierung* (Paderborn: Konstanz University Press, 2016), 23.

11. Robert Musil, *The Man without Qualities*, trans. Sophie Wilkins (New York: Knopf, 1995), 40.

12. Florian Hoof, "Film—Labor—Flow-Charting. Mediale Kristallisationspunkte moderner Managementtheorien," in *Medien in Raum und Zeit: Maßverhältnisse des Medialen*, ed. Ingo Köster und Kai Schubert (Bielefeld: Transcript Verlag, 2009), 239–266, 241.

13. Florian Hoof, *Engel der Effizienz: Eine Mediengeschichte der Unternehmensberatung* (Konstanz: Konstanz University Press, 2015), 11.

14. Hoof, *Engel der Effizienz*, 15f.

15. Andreas Reckwitz, *Die Erfindung der Kreativität: Zum Prozess gesellschaftlicher Ästhetisierung* (Berlin: Suhrkamp, 2012), 186.

16. See Jennifer Karns Alexander, *The Mantra of Efficiency: From Waterwheel to Social Control* (Baltimore: Johns Hopkins University Press, 2008), 2ff.

17. Kommission für Zukunftsfragen Bayern und Sachsen, ed., *Erwerbstätigkeit und Arbeitslosigkeit in Deutschland:*

Entwicklung, Ursachen und Maßnahmen. Teil III. Maßnahmen zur Verbesserung der Beschäftigungslage (Bonn: Kommission für Zukunftsfragen Bayern und Sachsen, 1997), 36. Quoted in Ulrich Bröckling, Das unternehmerische Selbst: Soziologie einer Lebensform (Frankfurt am Main: Suhrkamp Verlag, 2007), 8.

18. Katja Kraus, Macht: Geschichten von Erfolg und Scheitern (Frankfurt am Main: Fischer Verlag, 2013), 127; Nolte und Heidtmann, Die da oben, 14.

19. Jürgen Kaube, afterword in Niklas Luhmann, Der neue Chef (Berlin: Suhrkamp, 2016), 112–120, 112.

20. Helmut Schelsky, "Berechtigung und Anmaßung in der Managerherrschaft," in Auf der Suche nach Wirklichkeit: Gesammelte Aufsätze zur Soziologie der Bundesrepublik (Munich: Diedrichs, 1979), 20–37, 26.

21. Lee Iacocca and Alex Taylor, "Iacocca in His Own Words," Fortune, August 29, 1988, 38–43.

22. John Hendry, Management: A Very Short Introduction (Oxford: Oxford University Press, 2013), 24.

23. Candice Prendergast, "A Theory of 'Yes Man,'" American Economic Review 83, no. 4 (1993): 757–770.

24. See Philipp Schönthaler, Survival in den 80er Jahren: Der dünne Pelz der Zivilisation (Berlin: Matthes & Seitz, 2016), 82.

25. Henry Mintzberg, Managing (Harlow: Financial Times Prentice Hall, 2009), 1.

26. Schelsky, "Berechtigung und Anmaßung in der Managerherrschaft," 26.

27. Schelsky, "Berechtigung und Anmaßung in der Managerherrschaft," 35.

28. Ulrich Bröckling bases his analysis largely on management advice books. Similarly, the French sociologists Luc Boltanski and Ève Chiapello refer to management advice books in their large-scale study The New Spirit of Capitalism (1996),

comparing a selection of books from the 1960s and 1990s and drawing conclusions about the transformation of capitalism and its grounds for legitimation.

29. Schelsky, "Berechtigung und Anmaßung in der Managerherrschaft," 34.

30. Stephen Denning, *The Leader's Guide to Storytelling: Mastering the Art and Discipline of Business Narrative* (San Francisco: Wiley, 2005), xi.

31. For a critique of the World Bank, see Michael Goldman, *Imperial Nature: The World Bank and Struggles for Social Justice in the Age of Globalization* (New Haven, CT: Yale University Press, 2005).

32. By the beginning of the twenty-first century, the focus had once again returned to finance "because knowledge generation does not generally pay for itself," as former World Bank manager David A. Philips explained. Besides, knowledge management failed to make truly relevant knowledge available: "At the extreme, operations were taking place without knowledge, and knowledge was being generated without operations." David A. Phillips, *Reforming the World Bank: Twenty Years of Trial—and Error* (Cambridge: Cambridge University Press, 2009), 10, 74.

33. Denning, *The Leader's Guide to Storytelling*, 2.

34. Stephen Denning, *The Painter: A Novel of Pursuit* (Lincoln: iUniverse, 2000), 45; the following quotations are on pp. 48, 80, 12, 43, 9.

35. Eva Buchhorn, "Von Dichtern und Lenkern: Manager als Schriftsteller," *Manager Magazin,* January 2012.

36. Felix Philipp Ingold, *Autorschaft und Management: Eine poetologische Skizze* (Graz: Droschl, 1993).

37. Utz Claassen, *Atomblut: Ein Wirtschaftskrimi* (Berlin: Ullstein, 2012), 378.

38. Markus Balser, "Grüne Energie im Überfluss," *Süddeutsche Zeitung*, February 22, 2012, http://www.sueddeutsche.de/wirtschaft/utz-claassen-veroeffentlicht-roman-gruene-energieim-ueberfluss-1.1290180.

39. This quotation and the following ones come from Heike Kunert, "Der Pimmel ist ein Schoßhündchen," *Zeit Online*, November 10, 2014, http://www.zeit.de/kultur/2014-11/open-mike.

40. Thomas Mann, *Werke—Briefe—Tagebücher: Große kommentierte Frankfurter Ausgabe*, vol. 21, *Briefe I. 1889–1913* (Frankfurt am Main: Fischer Verlag, 2002), 89.

41. See Klaus Bartels, "Die zwei Körper des Dichters: Stefan Georges Arbeit an seinem öffentlichen Gesicht," in *Autorinszenierungen: Autorschaft und Literarisches Werk im Kontext der Medien*, ed. Christine Künzel und Jörg Schönert (Würzburg: Königshausen und Neumann, 2007), 25–46, 29.

42. Ute Schneider, "Literatur auf dem Markt—Kommunikation, Aufmerksamkeit, Inszenierung," in *Literaturbetrieb: Zur Poetik einer Produktionsgemeinschaft*, ed. Philipp Theisohn und Christiane Weder (Munich: Fink, 2013), 235–247, 243.

43. Walter Benjamin, "Krisis des Romans: Zu Döblins 'Berlin Alexanderplatz,'" in *Erzählen* (Frankfurt am Main: Suhrkamp, 2007), 55–60, 55; Maurice Blanchot, *The Space of Literature*, trans. Ann Smock (Lincoln: University of Nebraska Press, 2012), 25.

44. Roland Barthes, *The Semiotic Challenge*, trans. Richard Howard (Berkeley: University of California Press, 1994), 92.

45. Recently Karl-Heinz Göttert proposed a reading method that differs from Barthes's. After observing Barack Obama's 2008 campaign, Göttert researched rhetoric as a practice, not as a theory. In the process of investigating applied rhetoric and studying the speeches of individual figures, he discovered a line of thought that began in antiquity and continues into the present. He used it to fill out the popular understanding in

which rhetoric disappeared in the eighteenth century, experiencing a resurgence of interest only in the twentieth century, and then only from a historical perspective. See Karl-Heinz Göttert, *Mythos Redemacht: Eine andere Geschichte der Rhetorik* (Frankfurt am Main: Fischer Verlag, 2015), 9–19.

46. Paul Smith, *Lead with a Story: A Guide to Crafting Business Narratives That Captivate, Convince, and Inspire* (New York: McGraw-Hill Education, 2012), 55.

47. Karl-Heinz Göttert views storytelling as a modern, moderate form of rhetoric. (His example is EU Parliament president Martin Schulz, who likes to "enrich his speeches with telling 'stories.'") While traditional rhetoric is aggressive, seeking subjugation (in this sense it reproduces patriarchal gender relations: the speaker is masculine, while the submissive listeners have a female connotation), modern-day neuroscience studies have revealed "that listeners recoil from arguments that are aggressive or too direct." Thus, storytelling as a more discreet form of rhetoric fits perfectly with these findings. See: Göttert, *Mythos Redemacht*, 14–15.

48. Hoof, *Engel der Effizienz*, 10–11. Frank B. Gilbreth's "Wheel of Motion" is, as he explains himself, "not unlike the 'Wheel of Life' of Hindus." Hoof points to the fact that the holistic circle is to be found in the "McKinsey 7-S-Model" developed by Tom Peters and Robert Waterman in the 1980s.

49. Roland Barthes, *The Semiotic Challenge*, 43.

50. Friedrich Nietzsche, "Description of Ancient Rhetoric," in *Friedrich Nietzsche on Rhetoric and Language*, ed. Sander L. Gilman et al. (Oxford: Oxford University Press, 1989), 21. Nietzsche points to the fact that the idea of natural and non-natural language simply refers to two forms of rhetoric: "There is obviously no unrhetorical 'naturalness' of language to which one could appeal; language itself is the result of purely rhetorical arts." See Nietzsche, "Description of Ancient Rhetoric," 21.

51. Smith, *Lead with a Story*, 54–55.

52. Barthes, *The Semiotic Challenge*, 17–18.

53. Stephen Denning, *Squirrel Inc.: A Fable of Leadership through Storytelling* (San Francisco: Wiley, 2004), 17–18.

54. Michael Esders, *Die enteignete Poesie: Wie Medien, Marketing und PR die Literatur ausbeuten* (Bielefeld: Aisthesis, 2011), 45, 15, 111.

55. Gary S. Becker, "Economic Imperialism," *Religion & Liberty* 3, no. 2 (1993), http://www.acton.org/pub/religion-liberty/volume-3-number-2/economic-imperialism.

56. See Andreas Reckwitz, *Die Erfindung der Kreativität*, 55ff.

57. Markus Metz and Georg Seesslen, *Geld frisst Kunst, Kunst frisst Geld: Ein Pamphlet* (Berlin: Suhrkamp, 2014), 58.

58. Pierre Bourdieu, *The Rules of Art: Genesis and Structure of the Literary Field,* trans. Susan Emanuel (Stanford, CA: Stanford University Press, 1995), 228.

59. Albrecht Koschorke, *Wahrheit und Erfindung: Grundzüge einer Allgemeinen Erzähltheorie* (Frankfurt am Main: Fischer Verlag, 2012), 15. Emphasis is the author's.

60. Nassim Nicholas Taleb, *The Black Swan: The Impact of the Highly Improbable Fragility*, 2nd ed. (New York: Random House, 2010), xxxi.

61. Quoted in Werner Hamacher, "Echolos," in *Nietzsche aus Frankreich*, ed. Werner Hamacher (Berlin: Europäische Verlagsanstalt, 2003), 7–17, 7. In the interpretation of Gide's letter, I reference Hamacher's ideas.

62. Jean Baudrillard, *Cool Memories 1980–1985* (London: Verso 1990), 47: "In all things, one should only concern oneself with the effects"; Jean-François Lyotard and Jean-Loup Thébaud, *Just Gaming*, trans. Wlad Godzich (Minneapolis: University of Minnesota Press, 1985), 5. "Which means that it is not really a matter of arriving at the truth of the content of the theses of the book, but rather a question of coming to grips with the

new effects produced by the new situation. ... The effects that have been produced upon us will be constitutive elements of the new book." In this interview, Lyotard is referring to his 1974 book *Libidinal Economy*.

63. Gianluigi Ricuperati, "Dinner with Microsoft's Chief Story-teller," May 2, 2016, http://032c.com/microsoft-storyteller -steve-clayton.

64. Steve Clayton, "#Cannes_Lions 2014: The Art and Science of Storytelling in the Digital Age," June 10, 2014, http://blogs. microsoft.com/next/2014/06/10/cannes_lions-2014-the-art -and-science-of-storytelling-in-the-digital-age/#sm.00000 jgfgwwlgcd0zuk7vgv2ream3.

65. Lev Manovich, *The Language of New Media* (Cambridge, MA: MIT Press, 2001), 225, 228. However, Manovich does refer to a "database story" that exists only in scattered, unstructured segments on a storage medium and is brought into a narra-tive order only by potential users. In this case the story doesn't result from the principle of the database but rather is pro-jected onto the database in order to make the latter accessi-ble. By contrast, Marcus Burkhart has problematized the talk and conception of databases, arguing that we cannot consis-tently speak of them as such. He refers to the idea of a univer-sal or generally valid database as a "fiction" and a "fantasy structure" of data evangelists. See Marcus Burkhardt, *Digitale Datenbanken: Eine Medientheorie im Zeitalter von Big Data* (Bielefeld: Transcript Verlag, 2015).

66. Ricuperati, "Dinner with Microsoft's Chief Storyteller."

67. Tom McCarthy, "The Death of Writing: If James Joyce Were Alive Today He'd Be Working for Google," *The Guardian*, March 7, 2015, http://www.theguardian.com/books/2015/mar/07/ tom-mccarthy-death-writing-james-joyce-working-google.

68. Tom McCarthy, *Satin Island* (New York: Knopf, 2015), 17.

69. Gilles Deleuze, "Postscript on Societies of Control," in *Negoti-ations* (New York: Columbia University Press, 1990), 181.